April and My Classmates:

Growing Up in Small Towns of Northeast Oregon

Robert M. Vancil

Don & Roxanne

I hope you enjoy the stories as much as I enjoyed remembering them and writing them down

Bob

2019

Contents

Acknowledgments

My parents, Marvin and Merna, provided me with a wide variety of settings and experiences that I have always treasured, even if, as one of my sisters said, "You must not have had the same parents I had." Times had changed. Within just a few years it had become a different world. Looking back at the death of Donny, they held us close, but they did not stifle us. Thanks!

Through this time working on my book, Judy, my wife, was the consistent and loving encourager. She was my first reader. There were times she really didn't want to read or listen to me read the story again and again, helping me get them ready to send to my editor, Jami Carpenter. Jami really encouraged me as she worked on some of the stories and I saw the positive results. I was glad I was at the Central Oregon Writers Guild meeting when she spoke to the group as I knew immediately her sense of humor was on the same page as mine. I also appreciate my writing groups for their encouragement, even after listening to all my stories.

My sisters, Lynne and Dana, our kids, Mike, Steve and Karen, had to live with many of the stories being told and retold. Sorry, but thanks! Now I will have to work on a new batch of stories.

For my Powder Valley classmates, I know you would have really enjoyed April.

Introduction

April and My Classmates is a collection of stories, events, and happenings that were part of my experiences growing up in the 1940s and 50s, living in small towns, with populations of 1,000 — more or less. Most were in the northeastern part of Oregon; the one exception was North Central along the Columbia River. I lived in several houses and went to several schools, unlike most of my classmates who lived in one house and went to one school, grades 1-12, in the same building.

Dad's family was from Milton and Mom's was from Weston, about fifteen miles apart and just south of the Oregon/Washington border. Dad competed in sports in the high school, good enough to earn a sports scholarship to the University of Redlands. He came back to Weston to begin his teaching and coaching career, where he met my mother and ended up marrying her in 1938. I came along in 1939. A year later he was teaching and coaching in Enterprise and we made our first move.

We lived in Enterprise while I went through my first year of school. During this time, we lived in three houses, one in which a parent had to stay awake to keep mice out of my bed, or so Mom claimed. Donny, my brother, and Lynne, my sister, were born. Besides teaching and coaching, Dad became the principal. In 1947 we moved to Arlington where I started the second grade. In Arlington we lived in two different homes. In 1951 we moved to North Powder, where Dad became superintendent and high school principal. We moved into a teacherage, a very small house that came with the job. Of course, the rent came out of his pay. It was my home until I left for college.

Mom always claimed Dad was fired from every job he had — a little exaggeration — but somewhat true. He was never fired for the quality of his work, but rather political reasons; in one case, because this was during the Depression and he did not have a family, jobs should go to men with families. In another, during a game he refused to play the school board chairman's son over a better player. One time the entire staff was fired to save the district money, as they could hire new teachers cheaper. These situations caused us to move from community to community. I viewed it as happening to my family, not realizing the same was happening all over the country, especially after the war.

Life in the home was changing. At first, a few of our friends did not have electricity or running hot water. A few of my relatives and friends did not have inside toilets. None of us had TV until late in our school years. Chopping firewood and shoveling coal to burn for heat was common and an everyday task. Canning vegetables and fruit happened every fall. Few of my classmates had their own car. Most of my classmates had substantial chores to do before and after school. Washing clothes with a wringer washer, drying them on the line, and ironing them was an all-day job for moms. Dads had to often deal with flat tires, retread tires, and in the winter, sawdust or walnut tread winter tires. In the evening the kids in the neighborhood gathered to play kick the can or Red Rover-Red Rover before going inside to play a board game, then hit the books. Camping trips meant tent or no tent, cooking over a wood fire, sleeping on the ground, and maybe more work than any break from the routine. Besides, someone still had to do the chores at home.

Small towns tended to have some commonalities. The town took responsibility for the child. We could wander the town and almost every mother knew who we were and while we were in her area, she had her eye on us and our friends. She was ready with a sharp comment or a band-aid, whatever was needed. If we needed a scolding we got it and if it was serious, we got it twice as she had called our home before we had a chance to tell our side of the story. If we had a bike wreck, our knee was cleaned up and if needed, we were given a ride home.

Every small town had one or two grocery stores where Mom could call down, place an order, and I was on my way; hopefully, the items would fit into the basket so I could ride my bike and maybe swing by my best friend's house and he or she might ride with me. When I got to the store I would sign a carbon paper receipt. A copy was sent home with me and the original went into a file that kept track of the month's purchases to be paid after pay day. Cash was never used. The grocer or the butcher knew me, maybe gave me a piece of penny candy, then send me off with the admonition of, "Hurry home, your mother needs this now!" In one store, Dad set it up so he might purchase a six-pack of stubbies. The grocer would go in the back room, put the beer in a sack, and then bring it out to Dad.

The movie theater was a great place, especially on Saturday when most of us kids gathered to watch the latest Roy Rogers, Gene Autrey, Tom Mix, or Tarzan movie. The kind of film where the hero kissed the horse and rode off into the sunset after many chases and battles with the villains. A very important part of the theater scene was to look at the billboards for the coming attractions.

Before the main feature there were a couple of cartoons, a World News segment, coming attractions, and a segment of a serial. The serial could have been Flash Gordon or Sky King in a situation each week we were sure they would not survive, yet the next week we would find out that in some unbelievable way they always survived.

Every small town had a Masonic, Neighbors of Woodcraft, and/or an Odd Fellows Hall. Most were on the second floor while the first floor was occupied by businesses that had ties to whichever lodge owned the building. Most people in the town belonged to one lodge or another, and many belonged to all. The lodge was a unifying factor in the community. There was enough mysticism to the lodges that made it intriguing and brought many of us into DeMolay or Rainbow Girls.

The post office was the center for what was going on in the community. Everybody picked up their mail, every day. We had a box that opened with a combination. If we were picking up for the neighbors, we might ask at the window. The post master or mistress was a good source on what was going on in the town as they saw and visited with almost everyone who came through to get their mail. The post office was where we paper boys picked up our papers and used the counters to count, roll or fold for delivery. We had to be gone before the windows were open.

Most of the towns had a soda fountain, either stand alone or part of a café. After school and in the evenings, as we got a little older, we often met to visit, exchange homework, study, or just hang out. The fountain area was a great place to flirt or play the pin ball machine. There were a couple of taverns, and one had a pool table room that was a screened area where the young boys could come in and play pool if the adults were not occupying the tables. One of the taverns even had a shuffle board that ran along one of the walls. Of course, we could smell the odor of stale beer and cigarette smoke, but that was part of the lure of the place.

The railroad was an important tie to the community, too. It brought in the coal that was going to heat many houses and schools in the winter. Farm equipment came by railroad. It took out the lumber, the cattle, and the grain that had been processed in the community. It was a vital link. At the depot, beside the track, we could watch the passengers pass through in the dome liners and I wondered, when was I going to get to see the world like those people passing through, never ever looking down at us as they clackety clacked by?

Church was a part of growing up; most of us attended one church or another. The largest was usually a Community Church supported by the Methodist or Presbyterian denominations. A couple of smaller fellowships were part of the community and a small Roman Catholic facility held Mass once a week but did not always have a priest. The largest church always had a bell that could be heard throughout the town calling all to worship. Getting to ring the bell was a labor of love as it lifted us up. What fun! Our class's last real association with the Community Church was the Baccalaureate Service held the night before graduation. That night the bell rang extra long to announce to the world the new graduates were coming.

Our dads' jobs were in our small town or on the farm. Whether he was the butcher, the grocer, the service station owner, the theater operator, ran the depot, railroad track repairman, the coal and ice distributor, worked for the U.S Forest Service, the dairyman, hardware store owner, the post master, the house painter, the mechanic, the carpenter, the pastor, the teacher: this was their home. They supported the community and were the backbone of the small town. There would be no jobs with a future for us unless our dads had a ranch or farm for us to inherit. The rest of us were leaving, many to school, only coming back to visit.

Small towns, as financial centers, were dwindling away. They were no longer growing and they were on the way to becoming bedroom communities. For the class of '57 we were part of an end of an era. No one since has had the freedom of living in a unified community. I hope my stories give readers a sense of the freedom that we enjoyed and probably took for granted. Maybe we were just a light year behind the rest of the nation, but we had a grand time.

Enterprise

Early Enterprise

"GET SET, READY, GO!" Dad would say and the three of us, Mom, Dad, and I would begin putting puzzles together in a race to see who could get it done first. No holds barred was part of the game, though we might have put the puzzle together twenty times. We were racing to be the champion. It might be a puzzle of the forty-eight states or a 100-piece picture of an animal, whatever; we had three copies. The race was on!

Afterward, we read and memorized as we slowed down for the evening before bedtime. The first poetry I memorized were short verses written by my father. I could read quite well and I was expected to read to Mom or Dad. Later in the evening one of them would read to Donny, my younger brother, and me such books as Rudyard Kipling's *Jungle Book*. I had gone to a private kindergarten before Mrs. Scott and first grade. Reading before I went to the first grade was accomplished by pushing from my parents. When I was older I was expected to memorize famous children's poetry by H.W. Longfellow, Robert Service, Robert Burns, and Robert Stevenson. I also knew many of the famous authors and their works; we played the game "Authors" so often we wore out the cards and had to get a new set of cards!

Mom and Dad were very involved in my upbringing. I do

not remember ever being spanked, really spanked, but it's hard to believe it did not happen. Like the time I convinced Donny to get into the partially filled bathtub with all his muddy clothes on. Maybe that was the time when Mom said, "Wait till your father gets home." Maybe there were other times and I just have selective memories.

We spent considerable time outdoors, even in the winter. We had appropriate homemade winter coats and gear. We wore rubber boots until we were old enough to get galoshes, the kind that had snap hooks. We had a couple of sleds and I do remember Dad pulling Donny and me around during the long, snowy, cold winters of Enterprise. Donny and I each had a set of snow shoes given to us by Aunt Marie that we used to walk around our large front lawn. Neither of us ever became much of an expert at using snow shoes as we had a hard time keeping them tied on. We had many falls; Donny did not think it was fun to fall in the snow.

One time I must have rebelled, for I ran away with the preacher's daughter; we were only five. There was a Community Church just across the street from our house. The preacher's daughter and I often played together as we were near the same age. For some reason we took off to seek our fame and fortune or to escape something we had done. But in the tradition of the "small town," one of Dad's students recognized that we were quite a distance from where she thought we should be and took us home before a city-wide search was launched.

Many of our activities involved Dad's coaching, whether it was football or basketball. Mom was always in attendance at home games and many away games, so my siblings and I were there. The best part of big games was the night before. Dad would have the leaders of the team over to the house to make final preparations, discussing leadership and maybe specific plans. Dad had his philosophical basis for his coaching which was not just about winning.

Football in Enterprise was cold, very cold. Basketball season I enjoyed the most. Dad always let me shoot baskets after the game until he was ready to turn off the lights and lock the door. I can still remember the first basket I made and was so excited to show Dad how I had made it. Trying to show him, of course, I could not do it again.

Dad and I often went fishing. Fish was an important part of our diet. He was a bait fisherman and he always, when I was along, headed to the head of Wallowa Lake. He favored the bank along the north end and fished for Kokanee. The Kokanee was Mom's favorite as the meat was pink. Dad believed the Kokanee always came by in schools and the schools ran around the lake. When a school came by we sprang into action, catching as many possible, putting them into his willow creel, then waiting for the next school to come by. One time, after not doing well at Wallowa Lake, we stopped on the way home for Dad to fish Prairie Creek, just off the road from Joseph to Enterprise. He hooked and caught a very large trout. What a thrill. I could hardly wait to get home to tell Mom of the adventure, each tiny detail. Of course, she was excited when she saw the fish.

World War II was always a part of family discussions with a Europe map on one wall and a Pacific Ocean map nearby. Little flags were located on the map and the flags were moved based on the news. A frequent discussion revolved around Dad being drafted. Dad was born in March of 1910, which made him over thirty when the war started. During the latter part of the war he received a letter from the draft board saying he would not be drafted as his teaching was considered critical and he was now over thirty-four-years-old and thought he should stay where he was. I can still see Mom and Dad holding each other with Mom crying as the letter was opened in the coach's room. The letter had come in the mail at home during the day and Mom brought it to school unopened. How that letter must have burned a hole in her heart waiting for Dad to open it.

Like many families, the war affected our lives. Mom dealt with ration stamps to purchase certain items at the grocery store. Dad used stamps to purchase tires and gasoline. The inner tubes in the tires had many patches before they were considered worn out. Flat tires were a common occurrence and usually brought a swear word from Dad. Trips were well thought-out in order to have gas to return home. The folks were always bothered when then went to Weston and had to go out to the family ranch and get gas. The ranchers could get all the gas they needed to work the ranch.

The night of May 31,1944, I felt Mom shaking me. "Bobby, wake up and get dressed. Listen." I could hear an airplane in the middle of the night. "We are going for a short ride; hurry." She had also awoken Donny. Donny and I moved quickly, excited for an adventure. Lynne, an infant, was already bundled up.

"What's going on?" I asked as I was putting on my coat and all the time hearing this plane flying around Enterprise.

Getting into the car Dad said, "We are going to the golf course to add our lights to help the plane you hear, land. It is an emergency!"

Standing right behind Dad and Mom we got to the golf course and were motioned to a place to park, left the car running with the headlights on. Lots of people were there doing the same thing. It was exciting but kind of scary as I understood the plane was it trouble. Time passed. Suddenly, the plane, a B-24, came down for a landing. The plane was huge. The noise was deafening, shaking the car. Donny and I ducked behind the front seat and Lynne started screaming. It stopped farther down on the course. The cars started honking and we all yelled, except Lynne, who was still screaming. We were all excited to see the crew get off the plane. The plane was quite the attraction for the next couple of days. A year and a half later I remember church bells ringing, sirens wailing, cars tooting their horns as Enterprise celebrated victory over Japan, ending the war.

Our family had lots of visitors, both family and friends. The house was small and finding beds must have been a challenge. During the day, the men golfed and played tennis. Enterprise had the course in which the plane landed, which had sand greens and the men played with wooden shafted clubs. A tennis court was nearby. The evenings were wild with lots of noise and happy cheer. We all sat around the kitchen table playing games like Spoons, Old Maid, Hearts, Hell, and later in the evening, when kids were in bed, it turned to Pinochle. I always hated to go to bed and miss out on all the fun.

I also loved school. I had enjoyed a private kindergarten but was especially looking forward to the first grade, the 1945-46 school year, with Mrs. Scott and twenty-four friends. Many of the children had been friends in kindergarten. I could hardly wait to have homework to take home. Little did I realize I was going to have to wait around for many of my classmates to learn to read. I had been raised by parents who valued education and had a job that allowed them time to promote those ideals. They had established in me a love of learning and reading. They always had a book they were reading and often shared their stories. They expected me to have an appropriate book to read.

I was very sad when I found out I would not be going to Enterprise for second grade and would be leaving good friends. But the war was over, people were on the move, and we were heading to Arlington, Oregon, a small town on the bank of the Columbia River. New adventures lay before us.

Dad and the Globetrotters

"DAD, DAD, DAD," I yelled as I ran into the house. Each "Dad" was louder than the last.

"What is it?" Dad replied as he came around the corner. "What is it that you have to run in and not help your mother bring in stuff?"

"Mom said you were going to be playing basketball tomorrow night. Are you? Are you? Do I get to go? Dad, she showed me this poster at the grocery store, and she made me read it out loud and I had to sound out some of the words."

"Well, what did the poster say?" he asked.

"It said there will be a basketball game at the Joseph gym tomorrow night and you will be playing the Harlem Globetrotters."

Dad said, "That's right and I am sure you will get to go."

"I've never seen you play in a real game." And without stopping, "Who are the Harlem Globetrotters? Are they as good as your college team?"

"I suspect they are better," he said. "I don't know who the Harlem Globetrotters are but they are a touring team that people come to watch. They will be playing a team from Enterprise and Joseph." "They must travel all over the world," he went on and added, "I suspect they are from

14

Harlem, a part of New York City."

"Show me on the map," I asked.

As we went to the map on the wall, he said, "Now you know I believe they will all be black as many blacks live in Harlem." The picture on the poster showed a very large black man, with a name of 'Goose'."

"Have I ever seen a black man?" I asked.

"Yes," Mom said, as she joined the conversation. "You remember the town of Wallowa, where we watched your father play baseball? Many blacks live there and work in the logging business. When we went to California you saw many blacks but you may not remember."

"Dad, did you ever play against blacks?"

"Many times when I was in college and when I played AAU basketball after college."

Dad had been successful in many sports, but in basketball he had truly excelled. He was a key player when Mac Hi, in Milton-Freewater, Oregon, went to the state tournament in 1926 and again in 1927. He played for the University of Redlands for all four years of college and had played AAU ball. At the end of the season tournament he was named the most valuable player. He had developed a two-handed set shot that he used with deadly accuracy. This shot came from all the time spent in the nearby grade school. Being in a small gym with rafters, he learned to shoot through the rafters.

The Globetrotter game was to be played in the Joseph High School gym, which was larger than the gymnasium at Enterprise High. By today's standards the gym was small, so short that the center line was not the over-and-back line. The gym also had rafters that were high enough for basketball but they tended to be open beamed. The short court and open beams were commonly found in many of the smaller high schools in Oregon.

15

I could hardly wait for the next evening. The next day seemed to drag and drag. Mrs. Scott, my first-grade teacher, kept asking if I was okay and I kept saying everything was fine. She knew better. I asked her if she knew anything about Harlem. She said she didn't as it was about as far away from Enterprise as you could get and still be in the United States. I told her I was going to watch my dad play basketball tonight. She was pleased for me but told me to get to work.

Later in the evening we drove to Joseph. I watched the Globetrotters warm up. They were passing the ball and dribbling like I had never seen. I noticed that even Dad watched them and shook his head. There was "Goose" Tatum, who was tall and his arms seemed to stretch a mile.

The game was about to start and the two teams got into the center jump area. Dad was starting as a guard when "Goose" called time out, yelled "substitute" with a big show and grabbed Dad and pulled him to the center jump. "Goose" stood at 6'5" and Dad was 5'6". The crowd roared and the game began.

Midway through the first half of the game, Dad paused near the center line and launched a shot, his two-handed high archer. The ball went over the rafters, came down, and swished through the net. The stands roared as did the Globetrotters. Dad had decided to put on his own little show. I know everyone thought he made a great lucky shot that probably would never happen again. But a few minutes later, Dad did it again. Dad turned out to be having one of those nights when an athlete is just on and having a dream-like experience.

By the end of the game, he had made several half-court shots; in fact, a couple of times the Globetrotters fed him the ball so he could launch another. Of course, by the end of the game the Globetrotters had the victory and everything was as it should be. The players went to the locker room to shower while Mom and I waited in the gym for Dad. It became quite a wait.

Finally, Dad walked out with a couple of his teammates and the Globetrotters. I ran to get as many of the Globetrotters' autographs as I could, while Dad brought Goose over to meet my mother. Dad said something about needing to talk to Mom as we headed out of the gym to the car. I leaned in from the backseat where I could listen as Dad told Mom that the Globetrotters wanted to sign him to a contract to play with them. Dad also said he would be the third white man to play with them. I didn't think much about it until we pulled into our driveway and a vehicle pulled in behind our car. As we walked to the door, Abe Saperstein and Goose Tatum got out and followed us in. I could not believe it! I was sent to bed but that didn't last long as I stood at the door listening to Mom, Dad, Abe, and Goose talk about Dad playing with the Globetrotters and touring with them. After some time, they all got up, shook hands, and Abe and Goose left. I think Dad made up his mind as we drove home from Joseph to Enterprise. Even though he would have loved to play basketball for a living, he was under contract to teach and coach in Enterprise and he thought that was where he should stay for security and family. Sometime after this event we moved to Arlington, Oregon.

Dad continued to coach and play town team baseball. Often on Saturday or Sunday afternoons, the team journeyed out of town to play against other town teams. Fans often made the trip to support the local team and some rivalries were very intense, especially after some might have a drink or two. Always a competitor, Dad loved taking part but some players got carried away and thought they were playing for a world championship. I loved going, as the family always went, to watch Dad play ball. Even though he was my dad, I could see that in every sport he was just a step or two better than anyone else on the court or the diamond.

At dinner Dad announced that the Harlem Globetrotters were coming to Arlington to play.

"Do you think Goose will remember you?" I asked Dad.

"Doubt it," he replied. He also said he would not be playing.

I was disappointed, but to see the Globetrotters again was exciting! I had also been reading that Marques Haynes and Boid Buie were with them and I needed their autographs for my autograph book. "Dad, Will you help me see Haynes and Buie in the locker room so I can get their autographs?" I knew that Haynes was a dribbling wizard and Buie was a one-arm phenom who could shoot the lights out.

"Sure, after the game," he replied.

A couple of days later, the evening of the game, Dad left the house early to help set up. The rest of us came with Mom. When we got to the game, to our surprise Dad was dressed to play ball. Later he had told us that Goose said, "Marvie, you have to play, I remember you playing before and I want to see that shot, one more time." Dad played; he only took the shot once and it swished the net. The two men became friends and for a few years they saw each other whenever the Globetrotters came through. It was always 'Marvie' and 'Goose.'

On July 17, 1948, I went to see a Harlem Globetrotters baseball game with Dad in Walla Walla, Washington. They were playing a VFW Walla Walla team. They often traveled with another touring team, the House of David. The House of David players all played with beards. When they could find suitable opponents, they had a game but when they could not find suitable opponents they played each other. The game was a typical Globetrotters game with 'Clown' Ed Hamman providing the entertainment with his patented accurate behind-the-back throw from second base to home or throwing from behind third to first to catch the runner. We had a good time with numerous much-needed laughs. The family had not had many laughs having been just one year, almost to the day, since Donny had drowned.

Arlington

Town of Arlington

TODAY ARLINGTON, OREGON is a small town located on Lake Umatilla, a reservoir behind the John Day Dam on the Columbia River. Three major changes dramatically affected the Arlington I knew. First was the straightening of U.S. Highway 30, which allowed traffic to move by and not through Arlington. The second was the construction of the John Day Dam. Though started in 1958, it eventually flooded almost all of Arlington. The Arlington I knew was gone: the buildings, the streets, the school, the reservoir, our homes, even the hills were removed. The third was the construction of the highway overpass that allowed the travelers on Interstate 84 to hardly realize they were passing Arlington. I never knew this new Arlington.

When my family lived in Arlington it was a vital hub town located on the south side of the Columbia River on the main line of the Union Pacific Railroad. The Union Pacific had a branch line that went south and serviced the lumber, wheat, sheep, and cattle area south of Arlington in Gilliam and Wheeler counties. Arlington was on U.S. Highway 30, the major route east and west. State Highway 19 went south to Condon. You could catch the ferry at Arlington and cross the Columbia River to Roosevelt and join up on Washington State Highway 14. The location made Arlington a commercial center.

21

Other factors helped make Arlington an important stop along the highway. The town of Arlington, formerly Alkali, in Alkali Canyon, ran north to south, but to get U.S. 30 into the town, coming from the east, the highway had to go south in order to pass through and down the layers of basalt that characterized the Columbia River Gorge. Moving west, the highway followed closer to the river. Coming from Eastern Oregon, Arlington was about halfway from Baker City to Portland; each half took a day of travel, which resulted in a motel and two multi-story hotels and a few restaurants that catered to the travelers.

Arlington serviced the area. It had the RIO, a movie theatre, a Chevrolet dealer, a DeSoto/Plymouth dealer, two farm equipment dealers, numerous restaurants, a drug store, most major gasoline service stations (at the time), a couple of grocery stores, a soft ice cream shop, and many other shops and businesses that catered to the local people. A number of grain elevators sat along the river and railroad to carry commodities to Portland and beyond.

My family lived right in the middle of all the activities of Arlington. We lived in three store-front shops that had been converted into one large flat. Our three front doors faced the city hall, the fire department, and the Welcome Hotel. Our back door faced an alley opposite the backs of a farm equipment dealer, Marshall's Market, the theatre, and the drug store. Important to us was the small public library that was next door. I do not recall ever hearing what had been in the three shops.

Though not large, Arlington had a sense of a major city, being an important stop. I remember shaking the hand of presidential candidate Thomas Dewey as he got off the bus at the Welcome Hotel. I had my first look in a telescope that a tourist had sat up in the lobby of one of the hotels. We were able to go into the lobbies of the hotels and visit with travelers, the adventurous types who thrived on travel when travel was difficult and took lots of time. I had my first thoughts of racial insensitivity when a man showed me his limberjack dancing doll, and he kept using the word "nigger," a word I had never heard. That prompted a discussion at dinner time.

The department store flat was hot in the summer time. Very little breeze reached our home; as the wind died in the evening, the heat began to rise in our home. We really didn't have windows to open as the only windows we had were the big plate glass windows. We had screen doors on the doors, so later in the evening we might open the doors, but the doors opened up to the sidewalk, which left us with people walking by, very close to whatever we were doing. To cool off we headed to the river to catch the breezes. Once in a while we rode the ferry over to Roosevelt when we knew it would be coming back, as it was docked on the Washington side.

A number of activities helped create in me a sense of adventure and travel that have had a lifelong impact on me. First was the Columbia River. In the summer, almost every day we walked down to the river. We saw so many boats, with barges, heading down river loaded with product, mostly grain, I suppose. As Dad and I skipped rocks, counting every skip, we talked of where the barges were going. It helped me develop a love for 'The River.' We would discuss its flow, as no dams affected its flow right at Arlington. We talked of the Vanport Flood of 1948 and the people who were affected, why they were there and where they were from. Our discussions opened my mind to other parts of the country.

After skipping rocks, we would head home but we always stopped to watch the Streamliner pass through the river edge of Arlington to all points east like Denver, Chicago, and beyond. Oh! To travel on these trains would have been so wonderful and to see those who were traveling through the lighted windows, I was so envious. I wanted to be on that train, especially when they introduced the dome cars; the views those travelers must have seen! Watching the passing of the Steam Engine and the introduction of the diesel engine, we did not realize we were watching the end of an era and witnessing the start of a new era. We loved watching the station master, using a "train order hoop" to get messages to the engineer and the brakeman in the middle and another brakeman at the rear of the train. We always watched to see if the three missed so that the train might have to stop and back up to get the message. We never saw it happen.

The small public library next to our home was a springboard to me seeking to see the world. Mom and Dad often opened and helped take care of the library as nobody used it like our family. We read and read and then read some more. I remember even having to take encyclopedias home because I had read or thought I had read everything in the library. That included Francis Parkman's, *The Oregon Trail.* The classics of Robin Hood, Ivanhoe, and King Arthur helped capture my imagination. The poetry of Rudyard Kipling with "Gunga Din" and his storytelling in *The Jungle Book*, left me wanting to see these places. I wanted to see the world.

U.S. Highway 30 was our connection with the rest of the world. At least once a year Dad had to go to Portland for the Oregon Education Association meeting. Traveling west we headed over Rowena loops, a series of climbing and descending switchbacks that Highway 30 followed, and farther along another series of switchbacks at Crown Point. Crown Point was a great rest stop to see so much of the grandeur of the Columbia River. Late in the day we'd get to Portland, unless we went on to the coast, which Dad loved to do, even for just a day. We headed east from Arlington quite often as most of Dad's and Mom's families lived in northeastern Oregon. In part of the summer we often traveled throughout the western states as Dad attended coaching clinics. It left me with a thirst to travel.

The mighty Columbia River, the Union Pacific Streamliner, U.S. Highway 30, the library, and my folks created this feeling that I needed to see what was beyond our local community.

It was a very sad day when we moved from Arlington. I had expected to go to high school in Arlington and it would become my springboard. It was not to be, but some of the ideas I developed at that time never left.

House to Home

LATE SUMMER 1946, just before school started, my family was being led onto the property of the house we were to be renting. We saw a very large Victorian house setting on a bluff in Arlington, Oregon. It had not been painted for many years and the shrubs had grown up shielding most of the view. To a seven-year-old, it looked to be an eternal source of adventure, waiting to be explored, but not to my mom. I heard her say, "Marvin, what have you got us into?"

As the folks stepped up on the creaky front porch, I chased my younger brother around the lush, small but unkempt front yard, just a few feet from the bluff. I stopped, looking down at a pile of coins, large coins, like silver dollars big, a pile more than I could carry. I scooped them up, as many as I could hold and ran to Dad who had lagged behind Mom and the person showing the house.

"The coins are in the yard," I said breathlessly.

Dad looked at me sternly and in a way not like Dad said, "Put them in your pocket! Pick up anymore and shut up." I did! Later, after the renter left, the money came out to be counted. It would be used to pay for our food for the next month before my dad was paid.

We moved in. The house had many rooms such as a parlor, sitting room, dining room, den, library, and kitchen. The rooms were interconnected with a hallway. The rooms were separated by sliding doors with each room having two entrances. Each room had its own coal, or wood burning, pot belly stove. The bedrooms were upstairs with a wide ornate stairway leading up through the central hallway. The upstairs windows to the front gave a grand view of Arlington; the windows to the north opened to the school yard, which was to become our playground. The house was past its prime. Way past! There were two flights of steps of twenty each leading down to the street below.

The house quickly became our home. Mom was afraid of fire so no one slept upstairs. Upstairs became our inside playground. The den, the library, and the parlor became our bedrooms. Mid-September I came home and found my mother on the kitchen table screaming. She had seen a mouse ... actually, many mice. I do not remember where my siblings were, but I broke to get back to school to get Dad. He came quickly and calmed Mom down. As the weather cooled, the mice moved in. They must have had some form of communication, because they all came to our place, or so it seemed. Dad began putting tin can lids over possible entry sites and numerous traps were set every night and emptied every morning. Dad could not keep up and when I came home from school, if Mom was on the table, I had to empty or set traps.

When winter hit we found out that old Victorian houses were not well insulated, perhaps not having any insulation. Our living quarters began to shrink. First, we closed off the upstairs, then each of the side rooms until we were all in the dining room with our beds. We kids had a great time playing games until time to head to bed, like a big campout. That winter we lamented the fact that the folks had sold our sleds as Arlington very seldom got any snow; of course, that winter was the exception. As the weather began to warm, we began moving out of the dining room and back to our parlor bedrooms. The mice became less of a problem and I seldom had to rescue Mom.

There were two great features of the house. The upstairs rooms were huge and Dad put up a ping pong table on which hours were spent playing. Aunts and uncles often visited for the weekend so ping pong was played for most of the night. The second great feature was the school playground; all the apparatuses were ours to use. Of special note on the playground was a huge cottonwood tree, so very climbable that initials, years, and hearts had been carved into the bark and scabbed over. It was like looking at the history of the school and the town. I had to carve my initials.

We only spent one winter in the Victorian house, then time to move. We did, about forty feet down the steps to a department store house. Three store fronts had been combined into one unit. We had six big plate glass windows and three glass doors. The three former businesses were connected in the rear where the kitchen was located. There were inside connecting doors. The adults had the first store front, the center unit was for the living and dining room areas while the third front was the kids' bedroom. The back opened into an alley which serviced the other buildings and businesses on the block, mostly by truck. Next to the house was a small public library; across the street was the fire station and city hall. Also across the street was one of Arlington's hotels.

The move down the hill was epic. In order to save money, we moved ourselves, one box at a time. Up and down we went, all helping out and carrying what we could. It was brutal! I am not sure how some of the bigger stuff got moved but I do remember moving the refrigerator. Dad had a moving dolly from school. He was on the uphill side of the steps keeping the dolly and refrigerator from moving too fast while Mom and her mother, my grandmother, were pushing up from below the refrigerator to help keep them from moving too fast. They were backing down the steps and all the time yelling back and forth about how they were doing. I probably should have lost my mother and grandmother that day, but after completing the task they realized how absurd and dangerous the situation had been. It became a running joke within the family for years and years.

The mouse problem seemed to be solved as we saw very few mice, though Mom always swore she could hear them in the wall. The windows now opened a new sense of adventure. There were many black widow spiders in the webs and corners of the large windows and it became my goal to trap them all. On some of the easier-to-reach ones I let Donny help. We did this until he showed Mom the spiders we had captured; she recognized the red hour glass and knew they were black widows. She took the broom to all the windows.

Another problem, though, and much louder. At noon every day, the fire siren across the street was rung, and it vibrated through our very existence. On the hill we had been close to the siren, but now we were right across the street. Everything stopped, except my sister, who screamed.

The library became part of our existence as the folks had a key and we read and read.

Strange as it may sound, this house fit our family well. A lot of the action took place in the large kitchen. This is where we tossed and squeezed bags of white oleo to make yellow oleo that looked like butter. This is where board games were played, stories were told, and events of the day were discussed. The shower was off the kitchen making it the warmest room. Out back was a concrete slab where I worked on my basketball skills. Dad often had a player or two over to work on their skills and I got to watch and try.

All of this crashed when Donny drowned in 1947. I can still see Dad walking in the main door and looking to have aged a lifetime. The joy left the place for quite some time and it would be a couple of years before we were a happy family again, at least by outward appearances. It would take until 1950 when my sister Dana was born that the family was really back.

I was devastated that we were leaving Arlington and my last act of defiance was to go back to the old cottonwood tree and carve in my initials and 1951 as high on a branch as I had ever climbed. In 1951, Dad became the superintendent and principal of Powder Valley School District in North Powder, Oregon

Neither my mom nor I could believe we were moving to North Powder, considered the coldest place in Oregon. When the Union Pacific Railroad used to ice their box cars, the ice came from the ice ponds located in North Powder and ice was stored in huge barns of saw dust covered ice blocks.

We were moving into a teacherage, a house the school district owned that became part of Dad's pay. The teacherage was located across the road from the school, very convenient but too small, especially after the last two houses we had lived in. The house was a two-bedroom with a large living and dining room area and a large kitchen. A breakfast nook was on the side in the kitchen. A glassed-in front porch ran across the front of the house. To the right of the porch was my bedroom. To the left, a sitting area was saved as a spare bedroom. Once inside the house the folks' bedroom and my sisters' bedroom were on the right.

The plumbing in the kitchen and the bathroom had been added later so the pipes tended to be on the outside walls. That meant in the cold of North Powder we always left cupboard doors open and water dripping from faucets to keep the pipes from freezing, and on a really cold night Dad built a fire in the trash burner, a small wood stove, the only heat in the kitchen. The worst night was when Dad got up to light a fire and entered the kitchen and found a glaze of ice all over the floor. The water had been left dripping, but the cupboard doors under the sink had been closed and the drain froze, eventually filling the sink and running over the top. It was one of the few times I knew Dad was upset. All but the baby got into the cleanup.

In the main room we had a Zigler Oil Heater, which in 1951 was the very top of heating systems. That meant we had an oil tank outside along the side of the house. We did not have to bring in coal or chop wood except for the small kitchen stove. The heater had a fan system that moved the warm air from the stove; the problem was we all wanted to lie or sit in front of the fan, soak in the heat, and keep everyone else on the cool side. It tended to be a good-natured argument every evening.

My bedroom, open to the world, was truly unique, though I got some roll-down bamboo shades and a cardboard wardrobe box to create a little privacy. The window opened to the very first rays of the morning sun as it lit up the Elkhorn Mountain Range and later as the sun rose, the Wallowa Mountains would come into view. The views were spectacular, even being very early for a teenager.

It took a lot of blankets to keep the cold out, but I had a hot water bottle that I used to warm a spot in the bed. It did not last very long; of greater help were flannel sheets. I did get to hog the heat for a short time from the Zigler before making a dash to the bed. Very little of me would be showing, as I learned to get set in one place and not move around; I was in the only warm spot. I learned that if the windows stopped rattling, we had a blizzard; the windows filled with snow and I would awaken with a snow dune on the far side of my bed.

If the weather was really cold Jack Frost left designs on the windows that became spectacular as the morning rays created a kaleidoscope of changing light and shapes. In the summer the windows could be opened and it became the cool place of the house. A couple of dust storms had the same effect as the blizzards, a very fine dust that covered everything. I usually got help cleaning after the dust storms. But the space was mine; I had my books, my radio, my record player, my models, and my lamps that I had built in shop. I loved it.

Kite and the Wind

AN OLD MAN was walking down the road. Trying to keep warm, he had on a coat and an old hat. About that time the wind and the sun got into an argument as to which was the stronger.

The wind said, "See that old man walking along the road? I will prove I am stronger by blowing off his coat and hat."

The sun, not missing a chance to show off his power, agreed to the contest. The wind, being just a little greedy, said he would go first, so he did. He blew and blew and blew. The old man just kept wrapping his coat tighter and tighter around him. The wind kept blowing until it had no wind left. He had to give up. Turning to the sun, gasping for breath, he told the sun that was one stubborn old man.

The sun, taking his cue to begin, started to shine and shone brighter and brighter. Soon the old man loosened he coat. Turning up the heat, the sun watched as the old man removed his coat.

This was one of the first stories I read from *The Fables of Aesop,* a 1945 edition with color plates, given to me that Christmas from my Aunt Marie.

When we moved to Arlington, Oregon, in 1946, this contest between the wind and the sun seemed to take place every day. Located next to the Columbia River, Arlington was a windy, dry, hot place. Most of the time the wind came from West to East, blowing right up the Columbia River Gorge, bringing dust and tumbleweeds. We lived on the west side of town so from our perspective it was a great place to fly kites. I learned to fly kites from the playground next to our house. Dad and I sometimes went higher on the hill up the road that went behind the school house. This road led to the sports fields and the city reservoir. We usually flew the diamond-shaped kites with a Man on the Moon picture on the body, and they always needed a tail. I bought the kites for 99 cents and they often did not last long. The ones I really liked were the box kites but they cost twice as much.

When we moved in the spring of 1947 down into the three-store front flat, we had a very small back yard, a rabbit hutch, and a shielding lath fence that separated our back door from the alley. Dad conceived the idea that we needed a large kite to really test our kite flying abilities. That sounded great to Donny and me, but our question was how?

Dad took eight laths off the fence. Each lath was one and-a-half inches wide, a quarter-inch thick and four feet long. Donny and I agreed this was to be a real project. We were sure nobody had seen a kite this large.

"Why would we build it?" I questioned.

Dad asked us, "Why would we build it?"

After some discussion Donny and I decided, "So we could fly it over Arlington."

Was this possible, we wondered? Oh, the glory of it; the whole town would see our kite flying. But we had work to do. First, we had to sand each lath until it was smooth. We didn't want any rough edges that might tear our paper or fray our string.

We had to create cross pieces to hold the kite in its box shape, with four full laths making the corners. We drilled

34

holes with a Yankee drill that we strung string through to go around the four corners. Dad took Donny and me through the alley and into the back door of Marshall's Market to ask Mr. Marshall for some string for our kite. This string was not to fly the kite but rather to hold it together. We explained what we were doing and Mr. Marshall was glad to help. The string was on a coned-shaped spool that he used to wrap groceries and packages of meat.

Earlier, Dad had brought some butcher paper from school. We wrapped the paper around the four corners to give the kite its full shape. We glued the paper over the string that tightened the shape and gave enough rigidity so the kite would stand alone. Donny and I decorated the paper covering using bright construction paper. It was a great-looking kite that was so bright we were sure everyone would see it fly over Arlington.

Next we needed kite string, strong kite string. Around the house we had many parachute cords. Why? I have no idea or where they came from, but we had them. At the time parachute cords were made up of many strands of silk-like string in each cord. Ours were about twenty feet long. We took these cords apart and separated out a group of threads, then brought the group of threads to Dad. Using a special knot, he tied each group to the next. Mom, now in the picture, rolled it around an empty coffee can. This took longer than building the kite. The length began to add up and before long we had a lot of kite line wrapped around a couple of coffee cans. Dad built a bridle for the kite and then we just needed to wait for that perfect extra windy day.

Donny and I prepared some tissue paper notes to send up the kite string. They were four inches by four inches with a tear in the paper to hang over the string so the wind could take it up toward the kite. I had to write what Donny wanted on his notes.

Finally, a gorgeous weekend day in the spring of 1947 arrived. The wind was howling from the west. Perfect! Dad, Donny, and I headed up the hill behind our old house and got ourselves above Arlington. We were on a hill but we did not need to run; the kite took off and flew just like it was supposed to. We let out string and tried to maintain height but as the kite flew farther from us it kept losing elevation.

"Dad, what's wrong?" I could tell he was perplexed but maybe the string weight was pulling the kite down. The kite kept going, but flat. From our vantage point it looked like it was over on the other side of town, but in retrospect I am sure we were not as far away as we thought.

Suddenly the kite took off, flying better than it had flown, but to our dismay, the line went slack. The kite string had broken and as we watched, our kite flew over Arlington and crashed into the hill on the other side of town.

"Dad, what do we do?" I asked.

"Wrap up the string," he said, adding, "Donny, stop crying."

"We didn't get to send our messages." He choked down his tears.

Dad replied, "We will do it another time."

Thus began the tedious task of wrapping the string around the coffee can. As we walked down the hill, we began to pull in bunches of string; it was snagged every so often and hung over trees and houses.

Finally, Dad said, "That is enough." He cut off the string and we all headed home, all feeling very dejected. I always wondered what other people thought when they found the string hanging over their houses. Later in the day, Dad went up on the other side looking for our kite, but he never found it. It must have joined the tumbleweeds and tumbled along over the hill.

What a sad evening. At that moment the wind was no friend, though we were pleased our kite had flown from one side of Arlington to the other side. We were sure that many had seen our kite, but as it turned out, no one ever questioned us about flying the kite. Nobody but us had seen it.

The next day the wind was back and the wind and the sun had its usual battle. We continued to fly our small kites but the big kite faded into a forgotten project as did all the messages. No picture was ever taken of the kite and the three kite flyers.

A couple of weeks later Donny drowned and the kite project was never again mentioned.

The Block

IN THE SPRING OF 1947 we moved into the three-store front apartment. It was as if we had moved into an inner-city residence but in a very small town. We had the sights, sounds, and aroma found in the city, similar to when we stayed in downtown Portland. We could smell the food cooking at the two all-night restaurants just a half a block away. People parked along our street, day and night, going to the hotel. Car doors banging, motors starting, diesel trucks leaving their fumes, people walking and talking along the street, buses pulling out of the drive-through station were just part of the experience.

Our three front doors opened onto the sidewalk, though most of the time only the center one was used, the other two being locked. The fire station, city hall, and a hotel were just across the street. The library was next door and on the other side, across the alley driveway, was the drug store. The back door opened to a gravel area where delivery trucks could unload products to fill the shelves of the stores. The back of our house had a small warehouse that Dad used as a garage.

Marshall's Market was the most used and the most important to the family. Mom did her grocery shopping by the day. Whether she went or sent me, it was to pick up one or two things. The meats and cheeses were in the rear. Cheese was cut from a large round of cheese with a pull-down knife that cut a pie-shaped wedge. Produce was only available in season but huge squashes, cauliflower heads, onions and potatoes were usually in the front.

My best friend, Donald, was often at the store helping his dad. Bananas came in long boxes with many bunches in each box. We relished opening the boxes because sometimes we found a tarantula sitting on top of the bananas. The boxes had been fumigated so they were dead, but oh, the reaction with shivers down the spine. Just to see those huge hairy spiders was a thrill. We looked forward to watermelons being delivered to the store. Donald and I would carry them into the store for his dad and the farmer. On the last one, the farmer always started to hand one of us a melon but would drop it before we had a hold of it. Then he would say something about the two of us eating that one … which we did.

Karl and Margret lived upstairs over the market with two daughters. Nancy was a little older and Pam was younger. Our families became good friends; in the evening they came down the back stairs or we went up and visited. I suspect the dads had a beer. I visited with Nancy while the younger ones played. We both liked to read. She told me I should read *Just David*, by Eleanor Palmer. With the threat of death if I did anything to damage her book, she let me take it home to read. I had to agree that *Just David* was and has always remained a classic favorite of mine.

It turned out Nancy had a little more to be concerned about than me getting her book back. Her family's grand piano! One leg went through the ceiling into the store below. No matter how you viewed it, from the top down or from the bottom floor up, it looked strange. Her family was soon working on their new house out in the edge of town.

The back entry of the Rio theatre was close to the market. The back door was supposed to be locked but once in a while it was ajar. Sneaking in was always a possibility but that was kind of hard when Darlene, the daughter of the owner, was in my class. Every parent knew every student. What was exciting was out front.

For me, Saturday was the day for movies. I would likely get to go see the latest Roy Rogers, Gene Autrey, Tom Mix or maybe Tarzan movies, the kind of film where the hero kissed the horse and rode off into the sunset after many chases and battles with villains. I savored the news features as they offered a visual picture of the news from around the world. As I left I always stopped to look at the billboards of coming attractions, most of which I would not be allowed to see.

Gayle lived right across the street. Her father owned the Welcome Hotel. Gayle and I rode our bikes together all over town, down to the river, back out to "Dog Patch," up the hill, and all around. We were usually on our bikes. Once in a while we would go into the lobby and visit with hotel patrons sitting in the lobby chairs. They came from all over and most were just passing through, taking a day of rest. They might have come in on the bus or were traveling by car. Gayle and I kind of kept track of what states the patrons were from.

The school ground was just up the hill. where the regional marble tournament and a yo-yo tournament would be held on the playgrounds on Saturday, June 3, 1950. All were invited to play for the right to go to Jantzen Beach in Portland, Oregon, to play marbles or run a yo-yo for the State of Oregon title. I was okay with a yo-yo, but I thought my best chance was with marbles. I was eleven and would be playing others in my age group. We would be playing a tournament style of game, which meant knocking game marbles out of the ring without leaving your shooter in danger. If your shooter is knocked out by another player you give up your game marbles and are out of the game. I wasn't the best shooter but played the game well, picking up a few marbles and keeping my shooter safe.

As the game wound down, I was one of two left. My opponent left his shooter near the edge of the circle and I was able to knock it out and claim his game marbles. I could barely contain my excitement. It looked like I would be going to the state tourney, except that our age group was one of the first done. While other age groups were finishing, a family I did not know showed up. They were sorry but their car had broken down while they were bringing their son to play and wondered if he could still participate. After some time and discussion, they decided yes, he could play the winner of his age group. I was going to have to play this "foreigner" in my age group. I knew I was in trouble as I watched him warm up. He shot with only one knuckle down and generated twice the speed that I shot. He soon cleaned out my bag of marbles. It was murder! None of my friends had seen anyone shoot with so much velocity. No way was I going to state; he was a better player than I, "Gunga Din."

The Methodist Church was just up the main street. Mom made sure we attended. Most of the time Ernestine Hitchcock was the pastor while we lived in Arlington. The big lesson I learned and carried throughout my life is that a woman could lead a church just as well as a man. Though she was not in Arlington when Donny drowned, Pastor Hitchcock did help Mom through the loss.

Our house always remained the center of action, whether it was some of Dad's players shooting hoops and playing HORSE on our slab, carrying petrified wood from the petrified forest on the Washington side of the Columbia into the garage, a goose that was shot and happened to land at our back door, or a watermelon that rolled off a truck and stopped at our back door. (Neither the goose nor the watermelon were wasted.) During times of big crowds, like the State "B" Tournament held in Arlington, my sister and I had to move out of our bedroom as the folks rented out our room. It became a busy place.

Our center of Arlington had that inner city feel. My friend Gayle and I just happened to live in a small part of a small town that was much like the block near the Danmore Hotel when my parents took us to Portland. We were just a block from a theatre, a nearby grocery store, restaurants, shops, and the noise of the city that lasted most of the night. I was right at home.

Dear Donny

Dear Donny,

This is your big brother, Bobby. I think of you often and after almost seventy years, I must write to you. I have so much to tell. I believe we would have been a darn good team, much like our father and his brother. What bothers me the most is that I cannot remember the sound of your voice. I spend many a quiet time trying to pull your voice out of my mind but I cannot seem to do it.

It has been a long time, but somehow I feel I should tell the story and this is how I remember that day.

In July 24, 1947, we lived in the department store house in downtown Arlington. You were five-years-old and I was much older: eight, going on nine. Dad was in the high school painting classrooms on the west side of the building and looking up on the hill, watching for you. Mom was looking after Lynne, who was only three, and keeping an eye out for you. I was shooting baskets. Do you remember the basketball hoop on the back of the garage-like part of the house? You and one of your friends, a neighbor girl, were looking for Bird Bills, a wild flower that

43

grew on the hill. It was a little late in the season for wild flowers and maybe that is why you went farther than anyone thought you would. We all knew that area well as we had watched Dad coach football and baseball games there with many practices on the sports field next to the city reservoir.

Mom and Dad realized they had not seen the two of you for some time. As they started out to look for you and your friend, she came over the hill, running and yelling for help. She told them that you were in the reservoir and could not get out. Mom came home, looking and praying that you were at the house. Not finding you, she turned on the siren at the fire station. Dad jumped out a second-story window and headed up the hill to the reservoir, running as only Dad could run. He must have been like a fleet deer. Mom put me in charge of Lynne, told others at the fire station of the situation, and took off up the hill. The siren, I remember, kept wailing and wailing.

I called your name. I remember starting up the stairs to the school when a large lady, who said she was passing through Arlington, stopped me and asked what was going on. I told her the sirens were wailing for my brother who might be drowning. Looking up to the hill I could see cars racing up the road, bringing help to Mom and Dad.

What happened next can only be put together from scraps of information and stories that Lynne and I heard. The reservoir had a chain link fence around it; however, gaps had been left between the fence and the hill where one could go under, which the two of you did. We believe you decided to go swimming, not realizing it was not a pool but a deep reservoir. Mom always believed you folded your clothes, neatly, before you went in. She would brag how neat you kept your things. (You were not like your older brother.)

I do not know how Dad got inside the fence, maybe the same way you did. I do not know how many times Dad dived for you but I can only imagine his heart was near breaking. At some point a doctor helped Dad give you artificial respiration. You were later brought to the drug store down at the corner of the street. The doctor and Dad continued to help you breathe and you must have offered signs of coming around for they flew a Pulmotor from Umatilla to help you breathe. I believe they also ambulanced a resuscitator from The Dalles. All these happenings were over an hour or perhaps two hours' time. They did not give up on you until there was no hope.

When they brought you to the drug store, Mom, hugging the clothes you had folded, gathered Lynne and me on the couch at home to tell us what happened. We prayed for you, tears streaming down our faces. The three of us even sang some Sunday school songs of Jesus, the ones you loved to sing.

Some time later in the day Dad came home. He was a shell of himself, as if all signs of life had been removed from him. The minute he entered the door we knew he had not been able to save you. He was wracked with grief as we gathered together.

For many, many years I did not realize that Mom felt the blame was hers for not watching you closely enough and Dad blamed himself. He had lived a charmed life and could always make things right and when he needed it most, he could not save you. I do not think these feelings ever left either of them, though it dimmed in time.

I have to admit that, at that time, you were closer to Lynne than to me. Here I was, a big eight-years-old, involved with numerous friends in the neighborhood. I had a bike and a great deal of freedom. You and Lynne were close. A few days later in our nightly prayers, I remember hearing Lynne tell God that she missed you so much. He has had you long enough. Would He please send you home?

Your funeral was in Weston at Grandma Lena's church. Many from Arlington and Enterprise came to the service. Peyton Winn, whom we had heard many times at the Weston Pioneer Picnic, sang "Jesus Loves Me," and "I'll Be a Sunbeam," two of your favorites. There was not a dry eye in the place as he sang. Dad's grade school basketball team were the pallbearers.

You were buried in the Milton Cemetery. Mom and Dad chose Milton over Weston because the grass is always green and it isn't green in Weston. You became part of four generations of Vancils buried in Milton. The plot they chose for you, and two others for themselves, was near a newly planted maple tree; you know, the kind of tree we used to play under with propeller seed pods we would throw into the air and watch them spiral down. I remember them talking of the shaded area it would become. Over the years that tree has become a beacon. It symbolizes you growing up as a young man, maturing as an adult. Your roots are buried deep, your branches are spreading wide.

Missing and loving you,

Bobby

Arlington Fires

IN 1952, we lived near the corner of Columbia and A Street. The department store flat was right across A street from City Hall and the fire station. Every noon the siren went off to signal noon time and I suppose to test its operation. At our house everything stopped and the sound reverberated throughout our home. It was deafening! My little sister Lynne always started crying, even if we told her everything was okay.

Night time sirens were a different story; someone was in serious trouble. The siren wailed until the volunteers arrived and turned it off. Then we'd stand at the window and wait to see in what direction the fire truck headed. It almost always came out of the station, siren on, bells ringing, and turned left. Then down one block to U.S. Highway 30 and it could head in any direction.

One night when the siren wailed we ran to the window and watched the fire truck come out of the station, turn right and then left on Columbia Street. We knew the fire was behind us and was close by. We were allowed to go out the back door and look up Columbia Street. Flames were shooting out of the roof of one of my classmate's home. He lived just a block behind us. It was a terrifying experience to hear the men yelling, see fire hoses laying across the street, the flames lighting up the sky. Mom took me closer and I could feel the heat from the two-story house fire. It was so hot! The firemen tried to keep the nearby homes from burning. Later, I was so pleased when I saw my classmate and found out he was okay. His mother was hanging on to him and both were crying. Then I woke up!

The very next night the siren began wailing, the firemen gathered. The fire truck came out, turned right and the left on Columbia Street. I knew immediately the fire was burning at my classmate's home. Again, I saw the men yelling, fire hoses laying across the street, and flames lighting up the sky. Mom was scared and I told her my classmate would be okay and it was not long before he appeared in the street with his mother. This time it was real! The dream happened first and I know it is illogical, but my mind had turned the story around. This de ja vu event was very upsetting for a fifth-grade boy as was the fire itself.

During the time we lived in Arlington, the late 1940s and early 1950s, grass fires were a common occurrence. Fires were often caused by travelers flipping cigarettes from a car along U.S. Highway 30. Few cars had air conditioning so windows were open. Glass beer bottles and pop bottles were thrown; broken, the glass became a magnifying lens that would cause combustion, another big fire starter. Neither the highway nor the railroad had large cleared right-of-ways, so the grass grew close to both.The trains often had a hot box where the friction bearing on the axle overheated, sending sparks flying and setting the grass afire. Sometimes the cliffs along the Columbia River became a fire barrier but often the wind would move it by leaps and bounds.

The spring of 1949 had been very wet with lots of rain. The cheat grass and weeds had really grown and were tall and with the heat of summer, hot and dry. The grasses dried up and I remember the folks talking and being concerned about the fire potential. There had been many fires, all controlled, but the conditions were bad for a big fire.

Late in the day, the school year had not yet started, when the siren started wailing. We heard the volunteer firemen talk of a bad-looking fire to the west and heading toward Arlington. The wind was howling and bringing the fire toward us. The fire truck did not leave but men were jumping into trucks and pickups and riding out to the fire. I saw Dad jump into the back of a pickup and was gone. The dark gray smoke kept billowing and billowing. Mom was keeping us close. The sky kept getting darker; smoke and some ash started falling into the canyon where Arlington was located. Many women and children were getting scared as we stood in the street watching the danger coming toward us.

Then several pickups came roaring back into town and the siren started wailing again. It seemed like the rest of the men left in Arlington came running. Men were shouting, "We will have to set back fires if we are going to save Arlington!" Mom had moved up to the school yard and she and others were discussing whether they should get out of town. The fire truck was brought out and parked on the road that led to the sports fields. On the western, upper edge of town was a fence line that had gathered a year of tumbleweeds. Men started lighting them, running from one spot to another. We watched as the fire slowly grew and moved up the hill. The men then began spraying water on where they had started the back fire.

We heard the roar of the big fire and kept hoping the back fire would reach the top of the hill. Out of our view, the fires did meet on top, and by a very small margin, the town was saved. Much later Dad arrived home, his clothes covered with ashes and soot. He said the fire was racing so fast they could not keep up with it. Someone had shown up with gunny sacks and barrels of water; they soaked the sacks and slapped the fire with the wet sacks but they were just stopping little fires. They had no way to attack the big fire. They said it looked like it had started along the highway and the wind just took over.

A short line railroad ran from Arlington to Condon, which was the next town south of Arlington. Next to the railroad track was Oregon Highway 19, the two running parallel for quite some miles. The railroad and the highway offered little in the way of natural or manmade breaks. A hot box started a fire and it quickly spread toward our friend's home. The firemen saved their home but the house was left like an oasis in a sea of burned grasses, brush, and sage. The fire continued up the east side and as in all grass fires, heading east was good as far as Arlington was concerned.

At noon, New Year's Day, 1951, the Oasis Café exploded. When our six large plate glass windows dropped to the floor in thousands of pieces, we knew something was wrong. The family was in the kitchen and suddenly we heard the windows collapsing and then heard the boom of the explosion. Dad looked around the corner and everything looked okay but then he saw glass on the floor. In only a few minutes the siren was wailing, men were arriving, and the fire truck headed around the corner, just down the block. The streets of Arlington were covered with glass and people hurried to see if they could help. Mom, holding baby Dana, Lynne, and I headed up to the high school where we could look down on what had been the Oasis Café. Dad had gone there to see if he could help. The building was gone and many of the nearby buildings were badly damaged. It looked, from where we were standing, like a war zone where a bomb had gone off. I never ever heard what caused the explosion, maybe gas fumes build-up. No one was hurt as everyone was home on New Year's Day. We ended up with big sheets of plywood over our windows for a couple of weeks before the windows could be replaced. With just doors, our house was very spooky.

Fires in Arlington created a great deal of fear. Arlington had a lot of old wooden houses, fuel for fires was abundant and the wind blew almost every day. It seemed like the fire siren wailed constantly, perhaps because the siren was just across the street and we knew every time it rang, morning, noon or night. The de ja vu fire always left me wondering about my dreams, which were real and which were events in my mind.

Growing up I had other de ja vu events but none were as frightening.

Visiting with Family
(Umapine, Weston, Holidays)

The Airplane Ride

"SMARTY PANTS, SMARTY PANTS," cousin Richard and I yelled up at cousin Delbert as he passed overhead in an open cockpit Kaydet Stearman. He could not have heard us, but we could see him looking down at us with a 'smarty pants' grin and knowing he had gotten the best of Richard and me.

The Stearman that Delbert was riding in belonged to his Uncle Lafe. To me, he was Lafe, married to Delbert and Richard's sister. Lafe had been a prop plane pilot during World War II and had purchased two of the planes at an auction for a dollar apiece. Thousands of planes became available after the war, more planes than people to purchase them. One of Lafe's planes was to be parts for the better conditioned one. The Stearman was an open cockpit bi-plane, tandem trainer with the pilot in the rear seat, a popular plane for crop dusting and other slow flying situations like wing walking. This was like the plane chasing Cary Grant in the movie, *North by Northwest*.

We three were true buddies and in 1946, when my family visited, we roamed the fields and hills of Umapine, Oregon, as far as we could hear the bell ring for dinner. Delbert was nine-years-old, I was eight, and Richard was seven. Umapine is a small village located between Milton-Freewater, Oregon and Walla Walla, Washington, near the Oregon/Washington border. Lafe and Dorothy's home and barn were within the sound of the dinner bell range. We three cut across some fields and jumped a small stream to get to the barn. The barn had the two planes. What fun to sit in one of the seats of the open cockpits and fire upon 'Bubi' Hauptmann, an infamous German ace during World War II, who was credited with 352 kills. We were vicious in our attacks. When we saw Lafe, we always asked, "When do we get to go for a ride?"

Lafe's answer was always, "I'm working on the plane now, but soon."

The three of us knew the answer before he spoke and replied with him, "I am working on the plane now, but soon." And, of course, we knew he was not working on the plane while we were playing in the barn.

Then one day, maybe a year later, Delbert, Richard, and I got our wish. On Sunday evening we received a phone call that we would be taken for a flight on the next Saturday. What an exciting week! Every family meal featured some discussion of my upcoming ride. I am sure the rest of my family got very tired of the discussion. My little brother and sister were upset that they did not get to go. I was a great help; I told them they were going to get to watch and afterward I would tell them all about it. They and the rest of my cousins were too young to fly this dangerous mission.

Finally, the day came. I was up early and dressed and ready to go. We were meeting up at Delbert and Richard's home and then our families would go to Dorothy and Lafe's to see this historic event. I could hardly contain my excitement and I am sure Delbert and Richard were just as eager. When we arrived at the barn we were told we had work to do. We had to help push the plane out of the barn. It looked beautiful. I remember it being red with big black numerals. Push? We were ready! We had to step over and around tools. We even had to help pump gas into the plane from a tank that sat on a truck bed and had a manual, back-and-forth hand pump. We loved it!

Lafe had his own private air strip out from the barn. At the far end of the strip was a windsock on a tall pole. This had to be the day of all days.

There was no lottery as to who would go first. It was arbitrarily decided our age would be the determining factor. Richard and I argued over this decision, but we got nowhere. Of course, Delbert let us know he was the oldest with that 'smarty pants' grin of his. Oh, the urge! He got to put on the old leather helmet and goggles first. It was almost too much. He climbed in, without a parachute. Lafe double strapped him in while Delbert kept looking at Richard and me and kept grinning. Suddenly the engine sputtered and then smoothed out as Lafe revved the engine up and down. Oh, that glorious sound! Then they were moving, ever so slowly down the strip to the far end. There the engine was revved again, and suddenly, they were moving back toward us, gaining speed. The plane began to lift off the ground, and off it went 'into the wild blue yonder.'

They climbed and flew around in the bright blue of the morning. Delbert was so lucky and we both were so envious that he got to go first, but we were not concerned as it would soon be our turn. They flew out of sight and then flew back over the top of us. Suddenly the plane looked as if it were going straight up and then coming straight down, and as it leveled I could hear the rush of the air and the ear-splitting sound of the engine. A short time later, Lafe brought the plane back over the top of us, upside down. We watched as they did some rolls and came back for one last trip by the house.

As the plane came in for a landing, I got ready for my turn.

At that moment I felt like I was floating off the ground. Mom and Dad had grabbed me by the elbows, lifted, and carried me to the car.

"Why are we leaving?" I yelled as I heard the plane nearing the barn. "It's my turn!"

Dad told Donny and Lynne, "Get in the car!" in a tone of voice I seldom heard from him. Within moments we were all in the car and leaving Lafe and Dorothy's place.

"How could you?" I screamed as we drove away. "It was my turn!" I was furious; I was crushed. "You have ruined the best day of my life. I will never forgive you! Never!"

Barn Burning

"BOBBY, I have been saving these just for you," my Aunt Helen said, as she went to the cupboard to get out a Mason jar of watermelon rind pickles. Opening the jar, she said, "The first one is for you." Taking a bite, they were crunchy and tart.

She asked, "What do you think?"

"Aunt Helen, these are great. I love 'em!"

Most of the cousins, standing and watching, kind of shuddered and mumbled something like, "How could you eat those things?"

"They are really good and you not liking them leaves more for me," I responded.

Late in the summer of 1949, we went to visit Aunt Helen and Uncle Ernest and their family who lived in the country outside of Umapine, Oregon. Umapine was a small crossroad town, off the beaten path between Milton-Freewater, Oregon, and Walla Walla, Washington. Dad's sister, Helen, and her husband, Ernest, had five kids; Delbert, a year older, Richard, a year younger and I were the older guys, with privileges. Cousins Bethene and Christeen and my sister, Lynne, were a younger group while Cousin Harold was just a baby.

I loved to visit with my cousins. Their farm was off a gravel road and down a long, rutted lane. They lived in an old, large Victorian farmhouse with outbuildings that included a large barn, a garage, a milk shed, a chicken coop, a tool shop, and an outhouse. The front door of the house had a large window with an etched elk that filled the window space. That door was seldom used as most entered through the screened back porch. The house had a large veranda covered porch supported by large white columns. Inside were many rooms that I had learned did not have heat. Upstairs was a large area that had a pool table. Outdoors was a large picket-fenced yard that had room to play football, softball, and any other game we wanted to play. A tractor tire hung from a large tree. Cutting away part of the sides of the tire created an interesting swing where more than one person could swing at a time.

Inside, Aunt Helen worked in a very large kitchen over a wood range preparing a meal that included fried chicken, mashed potatoes and gravy with some home canned vegetables, unless beans or corn were in season, which were fresh picked and cooked. When we came through the door we knew we were in for a big hug and a look that would bring from her an expression of how tall we had grown and that we were almost as tall as she, which wasn't too difficult as Aunt Helen was not very tall. But she was quite round. Then came the watermelon rind pickles.

On this visit we had a while before dinner, so Delbert, Richard, and I set out to explore and to get some work done. They had chores to complete but if I helped out we would have more time to explore along the creek and just fool around. One of the stops was by the electric fence that surrounded one of the pastures. This was an exciting time to see who was the bravest to pee closest to the hot wire. The idea was to get someone peeing close and then shove him a bit. Since we all knew this we made sure no one was close by when we peed and then we would brag how close we came and surely, each one of us was the closest.

Some of the fields were white from alkali and were not suitable for farming. As we walked in the field the alkali dust covered the lower parts of our pants. We had probably been warned to stay out of the field, but we could see killdeer. The killdeer were great actors in drawing us away from their nests, hopping along on one leg, dragging a wing, faking an injury, crying as if they were mortally wounded. We didn't look for the nests, it was just so much fun watching them.

We watched where we were going and our stomachs told us to begin heading back as we didn't want to be too far away when the dinner bell was rung. We headed back through a pasture where the cattle had been and began tossing cow pies — dried cow pies — in the general direction of each other. When Delbert threw they tended to land right at our feet. He said, "Oh, I am sorry. I didn't get you, did I? It slipped as I threw it." Then he laughed and laughed.

I replied, "I bet it slipped. You just wait!" and off we ran. When we got to the barn the dinner bell had not rung, so we knew we had more time but we were now closer to the house.

Since we didn't usually get to go in the barn as my family usually left before chore time, I was getting a special tour. The lower half was divided with hay kept on one side and the other half was kept for milking. The upstairs was full of antique furniture and lumber. When Ernest's parents had died the house was emptied and the family furniture moved to this barn. Later the parents' house was taken apart and the lumber stored in this barn. Downstairs we noticed some old kerosene lanterns hanging on the wall.

Delbert said, "We use them in the winter when we lose electricity."

I asked, "Do they still work?"

"Sure," Delbert replied, going over and getting one. "I'll show you." We cleaned an area of the floor, with wooden matches nearby. We were impressed watching as he struck a match with his finger nail, lit the lantern, and trimmed the wick. About that time, we heard the dinner bell. Delbert turned down the lantern until it went out. He placed it and the matches back. We checked where we had been and it was clean, then headed into the house to wash up and eat. A large table was set for all to sit around. The food would not come out until Ernest was at the table. Grandma Vancil, who lived with them, had joined the festivities so I said my hello's and gave her a big hug. Soon Earnest was at the table, who greeted us all and we began eating. It looked to be a feast.

Midway through the meal a car came careening down the driveway with its horn on a steady blast. We stopped eating. The driver got out of the car yelling fire, a huge fire. The adults first thought he was talking of the house being on fire. Urgency set in and everyone moved to get out of the house on the north side. Aunt Helen yelled, "The children, get all the children!" Dad and Mom pushed and herded us out the north side door. Stepping outside we could smell the smoke but we could not see the flames. The roar of the fire scared us all. Moving away from the house we were able to see that it was the barn.

Grandma Vancil took us children to the neighbors, across a pasture, to the north. We all went, though Delbert, Richard, and I stopped a short way. Standing together we knew we had some responsibility in this conflagration. The barn was totally ablaze; the roar and heat were intense. Neighbors began to arrive, but there was no fire equipment. They began wetting down the side of the house facing the barn and trying to save other out buildings. The paint on the house began to blister and we were sure it was going to go up in flames, but with enough water and men helping, without any wind except the wind the fire created, the house and out buildings were saved. No animals were in the barn at the time, so they were safe.

When the fire was out, the moment of truth was at hand. The fault clearly pointed to the three of us. I was sent to the car. Dad had worked hard in saving the house, Mom had kept track of all the people so we knew everyone was okay. Dad went over and talked to Ernest and Helen. I do not know what he said. My sister was loaded into the car and we left.

I was sobbing and kept repeating, "We were so careful; how could this happen?"

Later, when we were in Weston, at 'Big' Grandma's, I kept hearing, "Bobby, how could you do this! You know better than to play with matches and lanterns in a barn." "What were you thinking; obviously you were not thinking!" "You know that Delbert and Richard are going to be severely paddled." I was not paddled, but I did lose privileges.

Christmas time came before we saw them again. I could hardly wait to see how Delbert and Richard had survived the anger of their dad. They had been paddled. Delbert kind of laughed it off; Richard was quiet about it. They had little time to play as they had to help their Dad survive the winter and it happened to be a hard and cold winter. The winter's hay had been lost. They were sent out into the fields to look for any hay that might have been overlooked. Neighbors gave some hay, but more had to be purchased and there was little money to do that. Times were tough and this was an even tougher time. A lean-to became a very cold milking shed. Both boys knew the family would not be having Christmas presents. I was glad we had brought presents for them all. Later, as we drove away, I was reminded of my role in their tough times. The tears came!

Christmas

"OVER THE RIVER and through the woods, to Grandmother's house we go. The horse knows the way to carry the sleigh, through white and drifted snow ...Over ..."

Mom, Donny, Lynne, and I would sing and bounce our way to Grandmother's house as we sat in the back seat imaging how it must have felt riding in an open sleigh. Then we would ask Mom what it was like. We knew she knew because one time her boyfriend, not Dad, asked her out and he showed up in a one-horse open sleigh. Dad wasn't singing but he would laugh and join in unless the road was slick; then he was all serious. The car was always loaded with packages and clothes for we were heading to 'Big' Grandma's house in Weston, Oregon, on the day before Christmas Eve day.

That first evening we would go to the Eastern Star/Masonic Lodge combined Christmas party, held upstairs in this old building with strange Lodge furniture and paraphernalia. A perfect place to explore, to open doorways that led further upstairs, where lights were hard to find and cobwebs hung from many items. The lodges always held a Christmas party for kids but as we got a little older, we were expected to perform. My first performance, in 1945, was to recite: "'Twas the Night Before Christmas." I loved the performing!

The best of the evening was the arrival of Santa Claus, when we each received a small gift and a sack filled with chocolates, ribbon candy, candy canes, and other brightly colored candies. The chocolates were a mound with a soft core, which were good except the pink ones. When we picked up our sack of candy we were also given an orange. The orange was pure heavenly delight and if we really watched what was going on we might even snag a second orange. We were never allowed to eat our orange that night, unless we lucked out and snagged a second one, because magically that orange was going to become part of our filled Christmas stocking. It took me a while before I figured that one out. I loved to squeeze the orange, cut out the stem core, drink and suck the orange dry, open it and eat all of what remained. I still can smell that orange aroma.

Christmas Eve morning we'd leave Weston to go to Milton-Freewater, Oregon, to spend time with Grandma Vancil, Dad's mother. Then late morning, we would head to Aunt Helen's place in Umapine, Oregon where we had lunch and we kids exchanged small gifts. Afterward, we'd head back to Milton, where Mom went into the liquor store to purchase a bottle of Old Crow, a cheap whiskey. Mom purchased the bottle as Dad, being a teacher, was not to be seen in a liquor store. The whiskey was for adult time Christmas Eve.

The day always seemed to go in slow motion — we watched each second tick by — then suddenly it was Christmas Eve. If Grandma's church was having a Christmas Eve program, we all attended. Grandma had to be there as she played the piano for the service, and then we went to 'Tiny' Grandma's house, where we had Christmas Eve dinner. 'Tiny' Grandma's house was small but it had a magical upstairs. Many, many cousins were there. In one bedroom was an iron-framed feather mattress bed that was so great to play on. At the other end was a wind-up Victrola with many, many platters. We had to be a little older in that room and there was no fooling around. This area was almost sacred. We also took care, as this area had open shelving of canned fruits and vegetables for the coming winter.

Sometime in the early evening I would slip downstairs and grab a popcorn ball. Tiny made the best popcorn balls in the world. Others later said they knew her secret, but they did not — no way.

Christmas Eve dinner always started with oyster stew, a tradition that had been followed since our descendants came from Wales. I don't believe there was ever a recipe passed down, but when it was made with whole milk, cream, butter, and great oyster crackers, who needed a recipe? I always went back for more. For me the dinner was an afterthought. We had ham, a beef roast, potatoes, gravy, green beans, jello salad, and the best homemade rolls, all having come from the ranch. This was followed with apple pie, covered with cream. As dinner finished, we kids would get impatient for Tiny to open her presents. We also knew that she had made something for each of us. True joy was watching her. She was so lucky; she must have had fifty presents.

Soon all the presents were open and we had to go to 'Big' Grandma's for Christmas in her home. The numbers were now smaller, around twenty, from very young to those in their eighties. Then it was time to open all the family gifts; a crazy time. Paper piled up and the noise level grew louder and louder as we all were having a great time. Later, we had time to check out our pile of loot. Many gifts were clothes or other necessities. One package, gaily wrapped, might have a pair of socks or my sister might give me a shirt. Books, board games, and jigsaw puzzles were always considered top notch. Comic books were read and savored, especially the classics. Then they were read again and again.

At this house 'Big' Grandma Lena was the queen and we all watched her open her gifts. It always evoked a response like,

"Just what I always wanted." Or maybe, "What a clever idea." Then time to clean up; sacks of used wrapping paper were taken outside where the men and older boys gathered to burn the paper in the burn barrel. We roasted on one side, froze on the other while we stood around the barrel and pondered the dark sky that stretched from shoulder to shoulder. The night sky would be full of a billion lights and I always thought of Christ and the vastness of what he had created.

Cousins and families headed home. As our home was too far away, my family stayed and hung the stockings, all which had been made by 'Big' Grandma when we were born. Now we were down to the final eight. I was the oldest grandchild so I had special privileges, like staying up later. My grandmother and I proceeded to look over all the lights on the tree; she said certain ones needed rotating shades. The shades had Currier and Ives types of scenes and if placed carefully on the lights, they turned from the heat of the light; another phase of the magic of Christmas Eve. Then off to bed and time for Mom to bring out the Old Crow and mix the hot toddies. Before falling asleep, what fun we had listening to the folks talk of Christmases past.

We got up early Christmas morning to check out the gifts. Santa had visited, filling our stockings with an orange, nuts and candy, just like we expected. A few small gifts might have made it into the stocking except for one big gift: the Santa present. Some years it was a sled, a winter coat, a wheel barrow, a toy box. The wooden items were usually built by my grandfather, an elf helper, while Mom or Grandma had worked on the clothing items. Two purchased items, very special in my view, were a carrom board and an 027 Lionel Electric train.

Breakfast was usually a smaller event as the kitchen needed to be cleared so the turkey dinner could be prepared for early afternoon. Some squaring away of the house took place. We kids were expected to play our games, read our books, and be occupied with our new gifts. Mid-morning a pinochle game was started. This game continued throughout the day, pausing only for Grandpa to carve the turkey and for us all to eat dinner. Different people played in the game, except for my grandfather; he was the constant in the game. We were all expected to learn the game and play. No mercy was shown to young players or learners. We learned to play well or we did not get in the game.

The turkey dinner had all the trimmings. Halfway through we wondered how we were ever going to clean our plates, which was expected. Of course, pumpkin pie was coming, along with venison mincemeat pie, though that was optional. Almost all the food had been grown, canned, and prepared in some way at the house, except for the turkey.

Over the years I have thought of this time, pre-1952. World War II and no TV was part of our time. Our extended family never had money to create extravagant Christmases, though all the fathers had jobs. The extended family was close because it was a priority of my mother and her sisters and their mother, my grandmother. We never had Christmas at home, except the one Christmas I had chickenpox and was too sick to go to Weston. We never had a tree at home until school closed for Christmas vacation and Dad brought one home from a classroom. That left only a few short days before Christmas. I never realized everyone didn't have Christmas like ours, the product of a small town, an extended family, a very inexpensive Christmas. That was truly unique.

May Day

IT WAS MAY 1, 1946, May Day! My family was living in Enterprise, Oregon. My brother and I were sneaking up on the house next door. Donny carried an upside down cone-shaped basket, one he had made from construction paper with Mom's help being that he was only five. My basket was square and I made it myself. I had used woven strips of construction paper to put it together. Both baskets were full of flowers that we had picked, early spring flowers, like daffodils, pansies, and dandelions.

Mrs. Denny lived next door in a large two-story Victorian house on a big lot that had a large lawn and garden. The vegetable garden was bordered by flowers. We lived in a small house on the other side of the garden. Early on May first, Mom, Donny, and I had slipped over to pick some flowers from Mrs. Denny's garden, except for the dandelions. We had lots of them in the lawn. The flowers went into the baskets. Shortly after lunch we took our baskets toward Mrs. Denny's house. Donny needed my guidance as we moved from bush to bush and behind a tree until we were close to the front door.

The front door had a bell twister to turn and make the bell ring, but first we had to hang our baskets of flowers on the door knob. I let Donny turn the bell and then we ran to hide behind a bush where we could see the door and thought she could not see us. Soon, Mrs. Denny opened the door.

She looked all around and said, "Who rang my door bell?" and then looked around some more.

Donny, who could not keep still, jumped out from the bush and yelled, "I did, Mrs. Denny, I did. Do you see the flowers we picked to put in the baskets?"

Mrs. Denny looked around and exclaimed how beautiful the flowers were and how great to have flowers hanging on her door knob. She invited us in to have some milk and warm cookies.

As May Day approached, 1947, and we were living in Arlington, I noticed we had no source of flowers and no one to take May Baskets to anyway. But I soon learned that Arlington had a very large May Day celebration. A May Queen and her court reigned over the May Day event with a May Pole and a parade and ended with a May Day dance.

The May Pole was placed in the center of the gymnasium and went, it seemed, almost to the ceiling. Many varied colored ribbon streamers hung from the top of the pole, fastened to a wheel. There must have been sixteen separate ribbons, three inches in width, fastened to that wheel, with a student hanging on to the opposite end of each of the ribbons. Each student needed to know his color, what direction he or she was supposed to go, and whether to pass under or over the approaching student moving in the opposite direction. Through a series of drills and dances the pole was wrapped and ended by being unwrapped. All of this was done with music and each of the dancers in costume. Each class was expected to have a dance and a routine and as we moved up through the grades the winding of the pole became more intricate and more complex. By the time I was in the sixth grade we might be single, have a partner, or even be dancing as a foursome. We created a kaleidoscope of colors and patterns on the pole. One year my costume was a mocking bird and we danced to "Mockin' Bird Hill," a popular song in the spring of 1951, weaving in and out as we wound and unwound the May Pole. The mocking bird costume was not Mom's favorite; she made my costume and was an excellent seamstress, but did not enjoy the project.

Arlington's May Day parade totally stopped traffic on Highway 30. Besides fraternal floats, farm businesses showing new machines, horses, the high school band, each high school class had a small float. It was a great parade, probably loved by all except those who had to wait for Highway 30 to reopen.

Dad was always a class advisor so he had a role in seeing that his class got its float completed. One of the early floats was based on the "Old Lady Who Lived in a Shoe"; I was one of the children who stuck their heads out the window. A later one was based on the song, "The Sheik of Araby," which conjured up a desert scene with a tent, a Rudolph Valentino type and a few young ladies with robes and veils. The real breakthrough was the music; the record was played over and over as I played the record from inside the tent.

The fall of 1951 found us in North Powder, Oregon. Dad was now the superintendent and the high school principal for the school district. May Day would never be the same; in fact, it had developed into a very ominous time as I became aware of the issues facing the United State: the Korean War, the Cold War, Communism, the atomic and hydrogen bomb tests, building fallout shelters, the Hungarian break for freedom and its crush by USSR, and the super May Day parade through Red Square. I saw all this in the news reels that were shown leading up to the main feature at the Eltrym theatre in Baker City. Little did I know they were parading through Red Square in front of the camera many times, but I know it became the talking point as my friends and I talked

69

of what war were we going to have to fight. As I was approaching eighteen, I knew I had to register for the draft and would be 1-A, available for service.

Memorial Day

THE SOUND OF TAPS floated and echoed across the fields of peas and wheat that surrounded the cemetery in Weston, Oregon, celebrating Decoration Day, May 30th, 1951, which became Memorial Day in 1971. It had been our family tradition to gather together on this day to prepare and decorate the plots of not-forgotten members of our family. Most of our pioneer forbearers were buried in Weston and became the center of our attention as each site was cleaned, decorated, and the person remembered. The family names of Lieuallen, Blomgren, and Adkins were to be our focus. We also took time to remember those who had fought and died in World War I and World War II.

Before the cemeteries were endowed for upkeep we had the responsibility of cleaning up our families' gravesites. Mowing the weeds, trimming the shrubs, and cleaning the stones were all part of the process. We wanted our sites to look good. We also took time to walk around the cemetery, read the stones, or help someone to find a lost grave site. A couple of my favorite stones included the phrases, "killed by Indians," or "Captain of the First Wagon train to the Oregon Country."

My earliest recollections of the time started with my grandmother picking flowers and saving them in wash tubs in the root cellar of her home. My grandmother had a huge flower garden, mostly roses and peonies, but if the flower was going to be gone by May 30th, it was picked and saved. Grandpa Bob had the job of getting the #707 cans (juice cans) ready with appropriate rocks used as ballasts and with wires bent ready to hold cans upright in the winds that were sure to follow.

Decoration Day was up and at it … early. Grandma's flower garden needed to be picked and put into the wash tubs brought out from the root cellar. Water was added to the tubs to help the flowers get through the morning. All the early spring flowers were going to be needed, especially the peonies and the roses, and if flowers were gone or had not bloomed there was Scotch broom from the Willamette Valley. Kids were sent out to pick bachelor buttons that grew wild down in the alley. My family arrived a day early to help. My mom's sisters and families arrived early the next morning. We had a great deal to do as over 100 bouquets needed to be prepared. A sort of assembly line was set up to get the job done. The list was checked as some people's markers needed two bouquets, one a rose bouquet and the second of peonies. To be specific, some were to be white peonies, others pink and a few, dark red. All needed to be placed in a certain order in a box for certain parts of the cemetery, in order to eliminate confusions when we were at the cemetery. Shirt-tail relatives, Grandma was the only one who could remember, might get the Scotch broom bouquets unless spring was off and we had no flowers, then everyone might get Scotch broom.

Cars were loaded and prepared to go to the cemetery. Being less than a mile away, some of us walked. Most important, the flowers rode at a slow speed so not to damage them. Once at the cemetery we needed to get right to work as the bouquets needed to be placed. Often someone talked about the person at whose gravesite we were placing flowers. The conversation was, "Do you remember when … or how about the time they ..." I wondered, "How does this person fit in the family?" or on these dates, "What happened?"

Before noon the sites were all taken care of, cleaned, and decorated. With a sense of pride, we were announcing to the world that our family had been honored. The whole cemetery went through this yearly transformation. A formal service at the cemetery was a military service. World War II and the Korean War were fresh on everyone's minds. A local pastor offed a prayer for all, the high school band marched into the service area and played patriotic marches. An armed color guard of veterans led a flag ceremony, placed the flag at half-staff, placed a wreath at the war memorial, and fired a 21-gun salute. A trumpet player from the band played Taps and off in the distance an echo answered.

Then while most left I stayed with my grandmother to walk the cemetery and listen to her stories of our family and her friends. She knew so many. She and I enjoyed looking at all the flags and fraternal markers placed at the grave sites. It seemed we could always find one whose fraternal organization we did not know it represented. The old markers and monuments represented someone's outstanding art work and were often found in family plots with low cement walls and many small markers with names and dates. It was a very nostalgic time for both of us. Being the oldest grandson had its privileges.

Then back to Grandma's house where lunch was waiting: baked ham, oven fresh rolls, potato salad, green or red Jello salad, and angel food cake for dessert. Grandma had baked the Parker House rolls the day before, lots of rolls, a huge pan full, and the angel food cake, from scratch, two or three of them. We still had more work to do.

After lunch, we went to the Milton-Freewater cemetery. Donny had been buried in this cemetery; a perpetual cemetery, always green and always cared for. The folks had purchased sites for him and them. Most of Dad's family were buried there and Donny became the fourth generation of Vancils at this cemetery.

Getting the flowers out was the first item of business. Donny had three or four bouquets, with one being the bachelor buttons picked in Grandma's alley. Two of the wind spinners were added by Dad. Each family, from both Mom's and Dad's side, also had little bouquets so the grave and stone areas were covered. We remembered Donny and discussed what he might be like now. Mom always picked up a couple of bouquets and took them over to a nearby site of a young boy, Donny's age, who had been killed in an accident; the site was seldom decorated.

After considerable time at Donny's site, we searched for Dad's parents' and grandparents' grave sites. We knew about where they were located, but as we all left, Mom and Dad stayed behind at Donny's site, and as I looked back I could see Mom and Dad holding each other up. Then they joined us. We always stayed some time at my dad's grandfather's stone. My dad would hold up two small flags, a Union flag and a Confederate flag and tell the story of his grandfather who fought on both sides and ended up being AWOL from both armies, horse-backed to California, then north to Milton-Freewater. It became a much-repeated family story.

Every year the family worked hard to honor our family, an important time, important to all of us as we worked and laughed together. Some days the wind blew so hard that most of the flowers were destroyed within a short time. Sometimes it rained so hard and everyone was soaked, but we were content knowing we had honored and remembered those of our family who had passed. Some days were glorious with the sun and the clear blue sky, the bright colors of the flowers and a slight breeze blowing the little flags. What a grand tradition!

Root Cellar, Woodshed, and Garage

IT WAS MY PRIVILEGE to spend extra time with my grandparents in Weston, especially during the summer months, away from school. The town had first been settled by my grandmother's family after coming west over the Oregon Trail in 1864. I would help out as needed, both them and my great grandmother, who lived close by. I helped with the mowing, watering the garden, emptying tubs from wash day, and getting the mail or a few groceries, or with my grandfather at the cemetery. Mostly I had time to hear the stories the three passed down. I thought it was a very special time and there were some really interesting places.

Almost every time I passed through the back-porch screen door I marveled at it. The screen door was a very old wooden door with lots of turned corners and bars. Every year a new screen appeared and was tightened with wires that crisscrossed from the corners. The wires had turnbuckles that allowed Grandpa to tighten the frame and keep it square. A big black spring slammed the door back in place. If I was told to get something that Grandma needed I went out the screen door and headed for one of three doors in the out building.

The closest was the door to the root cellar, the one where all the young grandkids slid down one time; a very heavy door, four feet by eight feet, that had to be lifted up. A rope was attached to the outer upper corner and went through small rope wheels. The rope then went up near the eave of the wood shed, turned and went to the wood shed's inner wall where a heavy house jack was attached to provide a force to help lift the door. When I opened the door I could smell the good earth and felt the temperature, which was always the same, whether it was cold or hot out. I walked down five steps and opened another door, an old household door that Grandpa had hung. Going down the steps and through the inner door I tended to wave my arm in front of me to make sure cobwebs were not hanging down. My flashlight led the way.

Entering, I encountered a new realm of aromas. The first, on the right, was the sauerkraut. In a very large crock, I could see the bubbling, fermenting foam that covered the work of the kraut. If this was my mission, I would have moved the foam to the side and use a large salad type of tool to dig out some of the best-tasting kraut ever. Then I needed to resettle the foam.

On some wider shelves were pumpkins and the large Hubbard squashes. My job might have been to bring one to the kitchen. There were multiple sacks of potatoes and if I was after potatoes I had to make sure I did not get the seed potatoes. These were saved to be cut and used in the garden in the coming summer. In this area, often hanging from their stems, were other root crops like onions and beets. There were usually four boxes of apples of differing types and each apple box had a unique aroma. Around the far side of the cellar were shelves where the canned goods were kept, all very organized: jars of corn, green beans, peas, beets, and tomatoes. And then there were the fruit jars: peaches, apricots, cherries, and pears. There were jars and jars of the fruit and vegetables, all in Mason jars, all ready for winter eating. Below the shelves of jars was all the canning equipment and getting it into the house was often my task. This included a large pressure cooker, with knobs to tighten around the top that allowed the temperature inside the jars to be high enough to kill the botulism spores found in vegetables. On the hottest days of summer we canned jar after jar and the wood stove operated full blast or later, an electric range.

One area had wooden boxes of Grandma's lye soap. She was especially proud of her lye soap. Everyone said hers was the best. I got to help her and Grandpa a time or two. Each load of wash would have a shaving or two of her soap. The kitchen sink always had a small bar of it to use if our hands were really dirty. We didn't want to have a scrape on our hand, though.

The one remaining wall, next to the door, had a pie safe that was used more for storage of jams and jellies. No meal was ever served at my grandmother's without a jam or jelly in a little server on the table. Her pies never lasted long enough to make it to this pie safe. Well, maybe for holidays it might hold an extra mince, apple, or pumpkin pie as she never knew who might be stopping by.

The second door out from the porch led to the woodshed. The woodshed's role changed from having lots of fire wood to very little as the wood range was replaced with an electric range and only a small trash burner was kept in the kitchen. But even though little wood was kept, it still retained the aroma of all the wood that had been kept there. It still had its chopping block, primarily used for splitting kindling but also an occasional chopping off the neck of a chicken. To the left were Grandpa's tools, all hand tools. He had been a finishing carpenter most of his working career. All were hand-honed razor sharp and were to be left alone unless he was helping us with a project.

In the woodshed were some galvanized wash tubs that came

77

out once a week, placed on saw horses, and used for washing clothes. During clear weather, a gasoline motored Maytag ringer washing machine was placed outside with the tubs to do the washing. In inclement weather the whole process moved to the kitchen and porch. Whites, lights, and darks were sorted into piles with the heavily soiled saved for last. The clothes were moved from the washer for the first rinse on to second rinse, each time passing through the wringer. The wringer, two rubber rollers that squeezed out excess water, was placed so the water would go into the appropriate tub. The water was reused for all the batches. This washer was eventually replaced by an electric motor-driven Maytag washer. Most of the year the water was used to help water the garden.

Hanging in the woodshed were many garden hoses. On days I had nothing to do, I would get down a couple of hoses and stretch them down the side yard of the house. There was a natural slope down to the street, and with a small ladder and clamps to attach the two hoses closely together, I would run them down the hill toward the street. I would begin building turns and more hills while both hoses stayed together. The turns and hills were shaped. Blocks of wood shims created banked turns and, using a sawhorse or boxes, they created lesser hills. It looked like a stretched-out roller coaster. Using a marble, I sent it down the notch between the two hoses, adjusting the two hoses just so for the marble to make it to the end. Sometimes I spent hours working on the track and at the end of the day, had to put it all away.

An old RCA Victrola stood in the corner, its spring broken. In the rafters was excess lumber for future projects. Boxes of flower containers were stored there to be used every Memorial Day. Suitcases, boxes of empty Mason jars, a few pieces of old furniture, a trunk or two full of old memorabilia took up the space that had once been used to store fire wood.

The third door from the porch went into the garage. It had a dirt floor. Grandpa kept his old blue-grey 1939 Plymouth there. Hanging on the inside walls in the garage were WW I gas masks, which, of course, I had to try one on and once was enough. At one time Grandpa had the Ice and Coal business in Weston. He delivered ice for the ice boxes to each household. The large ice hooks used for carrying ice blocks hung on the wall. Small coal scoops, for indoor use, had his ice and coal business painted on the scoops for advertisement. These hung in one area. Bottles of oil used in changing oil in the car were sitting along the wall. Old tires and inner tubes were in another area. The inner tubes had a value as they could be patched and used for the swimming hole or sliding down the slopes of the high school terraces. The most important value was in making sling shots. A few mechanical type tools were on the front wall as were the gas lanterns that could be brought into the house if there was loss of power during winter storms. I refused to learn to light any of the lanterns.

Coming out the back door were actually three more choices where one might go. Beyond the garage was the garden. First the rose garden that Grandma was noted for and kept in immaculate condition. Beyond the rose garden and into another lot was a huge vegetable garden. Both Grandpa and Grandma took great pride in all the food raised in that garden. I might be sent out to check a couple of potato hills for any new little potatoes to add to the peas I had just picked and shelled. While there I found and squished at least ten potato bugs. If I turned right coming out of the house I ran into the clothesline area. Long clotheslines with tall poles that could be placed to lift the line when the line was full of wet clothing and lowered when hanging or taking clothes in.

Across the alley right behind the house was a small shed that was used as the local air warden station, run by my grandmother. During and after WW II each airplane that flew in the area of Weston had to be located and an attempt made to identify the plane, then make a long distance but direct call to a central office where the information was recorded. Grandma would be in the house, hear a plane, run to the shed and fill the appropriate information on the sheet, and call it in. We had profile sheets and quickly learned the sound of different planes. This was a unifying force for many in the community. People in Weston would come and spend hours listening and watching for planes. Sometime later an officer in a uniform awarded badges and bars that indicated how much time someone donated to the project. I know I spent considerable time helping my grandmother and ended up with a couple of pins that credit me to the Air Force Ground Observation Corp. Thinking back, how did we think that Weston, Oregon, in the northeast corner of the state, would be involved in the attacks from Japan or later, USSR? At the time I thought what I was doing was important, as did all the volunteers.

My times with my grandparents remained a special experience for me and as I entered high school I always spent part of the summer living with them and working in the pea harvest. My siblings, my cousins, all had very special experiences with these two very special people but they have to write their own story.

Pea Harvest and the Greatest Game

I WAS SITTING DOWN FOR DINNER with my grandparents when Grandpa Bob said, "I hired Elgin Baylor, R.C. Owens, and three of their friends to help me with a building project at the cannery." Grandpa was the carpenter at Lamb-Weston, a large pea canning and freezing facility in Weston, Oregon.

"You mean Elgin Baylor and R.C. Owens who played basketball and football at the College of Idaho?" I responded. "Every high school football and basketball player in Northeast Oregon knows of Elgin Baylor and R.C. Owens."

"Yes," he replied, "the same." He went on to say, "I'm not sure they have much experience in carpentry, but we will manage just fine. I will have to teach them how to saw a straight line and drive a nail." He added they were the first blacks he had ever seen working for Lamb-Weston. He went on to say, "You don't see many blacks in Northeast Oregon."

In 1955, Elgin and R.C. had led the College of Idaho, a small NAIA college, just over the Oregon border in Caldwell, Idaho to very successful football and basketball seasons. Baylor, a future Hall of Famer in basketball and R.C. Owens, with his famous "Alley Oop" pass reception, were legends who were playing in our area.

I was in Weston living with my grandparents for a month, after school let out for the summer in North Powder, to work for the Bug Crew, as part of Lamb-Weston. With seven young men and an adult leader we walked the field swinging big insect nets, checking for aphids and creating a map of the area that needed spraying. Pilots were contacted to spray the part of the field that needed work. We started early in the morning and always finished mid-day.

Pea harvest was a big thing in the Pendleton, Weston, Milton-Freewater, and Walla Walla, Washington area. In the mid 1950s hundreds of college-age young people, migrants and their families descended into the area, whether driving pea trucks, helping in the fields, working in the canneries, or working at the housing camps. It was one of the first jobs to open up after school was out. The harvest needed lots of workers and even though it didn't pay well, it allowed for lots of hours. With camps, cheap housing was available. The migrants were 'poor whites,' following the crops from the south as they ripened. A month later the migrants and the college workers were gone and these communities would wait for wheat harvest in the late summer when many returned.

With our work over by mid-day, afternoons and early evenings were spent hanging around. In the spring of 1956, Weston still had a soda fountain hangout for teenagers, with pin ball machines and a shuffle board, pool tables divided from the main room of the tavern so we could play and a lighted tennis court with baskets on the side. At the tennis court we shot around playing horse or even a 3-on-3 game. We were average high school freshmen and sophomores, working on our game.

A day or two later we noticed five young black men, older than us, standing outside the fence watching us play. We stopped our game and invited them in. It seemed as if they were from a different world; what they could do with the ball was beyond what we had ever seen. And leap! We did not know people could leap so high. With one dribble, they would be across the tennis court and laying it in on the other side. What a learning experience! We all were in awe. I made sure they knew who my grandfather was, and they laughed and commented on how great and patient he was to them.

The next few afternoons and evenings changed what was happening at the tennis courts. Now many had joined us shooting and working on our game. Baylor, Owens and their friends came by every evening. People began sitting on the terraces, on the uphill side of the court, just to watch. No one had ever come to watch us high school kids shoot around. What fun, unlike anything else happening in Weston. It became the talk of the town.

About the fourth evening another group of men, a couple of them, quite tall, showed up to watch the action. It turned out they were part of a basketball team from a small, all white, Christian college in the South. It wasn't long before they came inside the court, shooting and taking part in the show. Soon we locals were just standing by the net, watching some great show boating. We were seeing abilities and skills that we would have to work on.

The next week Grandpa told me the project was just about finished and the five young black men would be gone. He and others in the community had heard about the court activities and decided that before they left, the high school gym would be opened and the two teams would play a game. He said we would be going.

The gym for Weston High School, though old, had close to a regulation-sized floor, had a center line, and did not need over-and-back lines. The backboards were wood, rectangular, and the key actually looked like a key hole. There were three rows of benches along the side. Very few people were sitting on the benches but my grandfather and I were there, ready for the action to start.

This pick-up basketball game involved two groups of young men: one black, the other white. There would be no referees and players were expected to call fouls on themselves. No clock would run, no score was kept; it would be basketball at its finest. That is what we saw; great individual plays, great team plays, shots blocked, rebounding above the rim, some dunks — the drop kind — not slams. Up and down the court they went to the entertainment of the few; what a fantastic game. When they took a break, Baylor and Owens' team came over and visited with my grandfather and thanked him for helping get the gym and working with them on the project. They played a second session, which was more of the same aerobatic action. If scores had been kept, the Baylor/Owens team would have been the winner, but the real winners were my grandfather and me. We had witnessed a game that we both would long remember and in our book, one of the greatest. The next day the carpentry job was finished, and Grandpa's crew was gone.

A football season later we knew that R.C. Owens was back at the College of Idaho playing football and later drafted in 1957 by the San Francisco Forty-niners of the NFL and the Minneapolis Lakers of the NBA. A year went by before we knew what happened to Elgin Baylor. He was playing college ball for the University of Seattle. He led them to the finals of the NCAA, was named Most Valuable Player, drafted by the Minneapolis Lakers of the NBA, and went on to star for the Lakers.

As my grandfather aged, he got TV in 1957, and watched a lot of sports, keeping track of his two favorite sports stars. He always loved to tell the story of working with Elgin Baylor and R.C. Owens. He took some credit for teaching them to drive a nail and to saw a straight line and maybe, helping them develop a strong work ethic. I got to say that I played basketball with Elgin Baylor and R.C. Owens.

North Powder

Town of North Powder

IN THE SUMMER OF 1951, when I was almost thirteen, going into the seventh grade, we moved to North Powder, a small town located in Baker Valley. At the north end of the Baker Valley, it had great views of the Wallowa Mountains and the Elkhorn Range of the Blue Mountains, about half way between Baker and La Grande. We were moving into a teacherage located across the street from the three-story school building that housed all grades 1-12.

The teacherage came as part of the pay for Dad's new job as superintendent/principal of the Powder Valley School District. The house was small but I had a bedroom to myself, albeit with windows on three sides.

I had not wanted to move to North Powder as all my friends were in Arlington where we had just left. In a half hour I had ridden over all the streets of Powder and I did not like what I had seen. I went home and complained that this town did not even have a movie theatre; it did not have a soda fountain and I saw no other kids my age. I was ready to move, now, and I reminded my parents that Mom complained about North Powder being the coldest place in the state of Oregon. But we didn't move!

North Powder was about eight blocks long and five blocks wide with U.S. Highway 30 passing through the heart of downtown. The Union Pacific Railroad was on one side of town and just beyond the tracks, the North Powder River ran its course. Surrounding the town were fields of hay or grazing land for cattle. Two small saw mills operated as the logs were brought from the Ponderosa forests of the Elkhorn Range.

North Powder did not have a good reputation, but it had an interesting history. Thirteen saloons once lined the street. Cattle drives brought the cows through the center of town right to the railroad holding pens. Ice was sawn and kept in the warehouses for Union Pacific. From the warehouses the ice went onto the railcars and transported through the Union Pacific system in their refrigerated cars. When we arrived in North Powder, just the remnants of this early time were left.

There was a meat market, two grocery stores, a post office, a café, telephone office, three taverns, a railroad depot where you could catch the local train, a coal and oil distributor, and two service stations. I hated this town! There were a number of large, sandstone constructed buildings, one with a farm buggy on its roof. One other was a two-story Masonic hall, the bottom floor stood empty while the Masons used the upper floor. There were three churches: Methodist, Nazarene, and Catholic. The U.S. Forest Service had a compound on the north side of town. The one saving grace was it had a library; small, but still a library.

Jimmy lived down the street, but he was a year or two older. My parents became friends with Bill and Vivian whose son, Billy, was my age. They lived on the opposite edge of town from our house. Several of my classmates lived in town but I was told they would be working in the hay fields or with cattle until school started. How was I ever going to survive? Eventually things began to stir around the school as more and more people began showing up. There was some life.

Then my seventh-grade teacher and his family moved in to the teacherage next to us. My anticipation that had begun to develop took a huge nosedive. Next door? How could I possibly survive? It turned better a day or two later when my teacher asked if I wanted to play catch, as he only had young daughters.

By the time school started North Powder was beginning to grow on me. I had a few friends, I had met most of my classmates and most important, I was free to go anyplace I wanted around town. Mom was taking care of Dana, my little sister, and Lynne was old enough that I did not have to deal with her, giving me even more freedom.

Before I knew it, six years had gone by and I was graduating. North Powder was my home town. I knew most of the people in the town. The town had lost the meat market, the telephone office, one of the taverns, and one of the sawmills. It was continuing to shrink. U.S Highway 30 no longer passed through town. The railroad still had freight work but no passenger service.

Powder Valley High changed. There was a steady decline in enrollment and by the time I was a senior there were only about fifty students. We dropped from eleven-man football to six-man football, which meant a big change in alignment of schools we played and it allowed us to scrimmage. That year the school voted to change the school colors to powder blue and white, but we kept the mighty Badger as our mascot.

We students changed, too. We were much more mobile as some of my classmates had their own cars and drove themselves to school. The rest of us had ready access to our parents' cars. This made Baker a very important part of our lives as we could date Baker girls, theaters were now available … and that included the drive-in. Billy and I had joined the Baker Chapter of DeMolay, attended dances at Grange Halls around the county. Chandler Corner, where so many had been killed, became a warning from our parents to slow down. No longer did we have to go to Baker only on Saturday to get a haircut; we could go any day of the week and many evenings we might go to drive the gut or get a hamburger and a coke in Baker. The relationship of time to distance had changed.

However, North Powder just got older and the farm buggy still sat on the top of the Hudelson sandstone building that had been built in 1900.

The Bike

"FASTER, MOM, FASTER!" I yelled. "I want to go faster." Dad was sitting on the large merry-go-round holding my bike up as Mom pushed the merry-go-round. I was learning to ride on my new, mid-sized, blue and white Columbia bike.

Mom said, "Marvin, are you sure this is okay?"

Dad responded with a chuckle and a smile. "It's an experiment; if he wants to ride his bike on the playground, this seems to be the perfect way. Just forget," he went on, "about the rock wall cliff."

"We're not that close," I tell Mom.

The school playground was where my brother Donny and I rode our bikes. We both learned from Dad's technique. Soon we learned to ride our bikes hanging on to the merry-go-round with one hand and steering with the other hand. Mom was always worried we would go over the rock wall cliff but we never did. The playground was a great place to ride; next to our house, it was hard packed enough to make for easy riding and a good place to slide our bikes to a skidding stop.

Next year we moved off the hill and down on the flat across from the Arlington City Hall. I now had the streets of Arlington to ride. A whole new world had opened for me, I could now ride most of the streets, except U.S. Highway 30, which passed right through the center of town. Besides riding, I developed an interest in comic books and purchased them with my allowance. On the back cover of almost every comic book was an advertisement for a Schwinn Black Panther bike. I could not stop looking at all of the features and showing them to Mom and Dad. I got these responses: *save your money, the bike you have just fits you, you are not old enough for the big bike, it costs way too much, and then we will have to get one for your sister.* These were some of the reasons the bike and I were not going to happen. I would have to be satisfied with my Columbia.

We lived in an apartment building a block off Highway 30. Across the street was the side of the Welcome Hotel. The owner's daughter, Gayle, and I rode our bikes all over town and we were on our bikes most of the day. We both had free run except having to push our bikes across Highway 30. We were allowed to ride down to the Columbia River or out south to 'Dogpatch,' an area of small surplus housing and even on South on Oregon Highway 19.

In May, 1948, we were riding and saw a small box was on the highway. We both rode over to it, stopped shortly, arguing what was in the box. Finally, I prevailed and we rode on. On our way back, we found 'Squirt' pop decals all over the highway. Gayle was furious with me and as we hustled around trying to pick up as many as we could, she let me know we had lost out on all the 'Squirt' decals in prime condition, if we had only picked them up when they were safe in the box.

As we came back into town, we ended up following a bus, like a Greyhound bus. We followed it to the street separating our two homes. A group of men were waiting to greet the person getting off the bus. Leaning our bikes on the hotel, we crowded our way to the front. As we got there the door opened, a mustached man stepped down, reached down, and shook our hands saying, "Hello, young lady." and "Hello, young man." Laughing, he said, "I hope you vote for me." When he turned his attention to the crowd, Gayle asked me, "Who was that man?"

I replied, "He is Thomas Dewey and he wants to be President of the United States."

Gayle said, "Oh!" and off we went to get our bikes.

In the summer of 1950, Gayle came out of the side door of the hotel, stopped, and yelled, "Bobby Vancil, you are the luckiest boy in the world!" I stood in front of our apartment house, astraddle my own Schwinn Black Panther, beaming as I tooted the horn to let Gayle know I was ready to ride. My Schwinn Black Panther had all the great things that came with a Schwinn. It had a rear Bendix brake, white sidewall tires, a front fender headlight and rear taillight built into the carrier rack, a horn in the tank, painted sinister black with lots of chrome and most importantly, a knee action spring attached to the front fork that smoothed out the bumps. What a sight to behold! A couple of hours later I even let Gayle try it out after promises of her extreme care.

In the fall of 1951 the family moved to North Powder, Oregon. Like Arlington, the town was divided by U.S. Highway 30. I had many streets to ride on with all types of surfaces and the knee action spring was great for all the roads. There were some hills in North Powder but I learned to avoid the steep ones unless I was going down them. Later in the fall I started to deliver the *Portland Oregonian* and the *Walla Walla Bulletin* newspapers. I needed a basket to keep the *Bulletins* in while the *Oregonians* went into saddle bags over the back rack.

Winter came early to Powder, which meant snow. Only major roads were plowed, but I still needed to deliver my papers in the morning before school. To combat the snow on the road I wrapped my tires with wire, tight enough so the wire did not damage the fenders but not so tight to harm the tires. Jimmy, who lived down the street, but a year older, taught me how to wrap my tires. The wrapping gave some traction and was kept on the bike through the winter with minor adjustments each day. In the spring the wire came off and mud flaps were added to both fenders for protection for the late wet snow and spring mud. Flat tires were a common problem and the tubes ended up with many patches. We could always fix our tubes at Marsing Garage if we kept out of the way. I am sure it was good for business because our parents bought gas there.

On one very special ride, my best friend, Billy, and I rode our bikes out to his grandparents who lived in the Muddy Creek area, about four miles out of Powder. We had lunch with his grandparents and started home. Being a very hot day an afternoon storm came up over the mountain. A rain and squall line developed as we peddled along, moving right with us. We could speed up and be on hot dry pavement or we could slow down and be in a drenching rain. We moved back and forth along the squall line, alternating between the dry side and the wet side. Lightning flashed close by and thunder crashed over the top of us. We were both yelling at the top of our lungs for the fun and the excitement we were experiencing. What a great four-mile ride home.

The bike took me hunting and shooting at the dump. It took me down to the North Powder River to go fishing. It took me by the twins and to where I could find willow whistle stock. It took me through the town delivering papers, collecting for the papers through all kinds of weather. It took me to the store when Mom needed something picked up out of the locker or something from the store. It took me to my classmates and friends, most who lived on ranches out of town. It took me by April's home, many, many times. That Schwinn Black Panther was an integral part of my life.

Neither the horn nor the lights still worked but that knee action was great.

The Cold and Dark of North Powder

"DAMN, IT'S COLD OUT HERE," I yelled.

A moment later I heard my sister say, "Bobby, I heard you say a bad word and I am going to tell Daddy what you said."

"Well, you might as well tell him twice and tell Mom, too, because it is damn cold out here."

We were headed to our friends who sold us fresh whole milk, the milk with real cream on the top, thick cream. I pulled a Flexible Flyer sled with my sister riding. She was to hold the box that would hold the gallon jar of raw milk. We had four blocks to cover, one way. The temperature was many degrees below zero. The snow was frozen and it crunched loudly as I walked and pulled the sled. After dinner, early evening, the dark surroundings were black, very black.

The storm had started a couple of nights before. It had snowed nearly a foot. Then the wild howling wind came up and we were in the middle of a terrible blizzard. Since I slept in a glassed-in front porch, I was always the first in my family to know that a blizzard had hit. The windows, single-paned and not very tight, which allowed the wind to rattle the loosely fitted panes. That was my wake-up call to crawl deeper into the bed. After a couple of hours, the rattling would stop as the snow would blow and pack around the glass, quieting the windows. This storm lasted a day and a half before blowing itself out creating snowdrifts, which meant no school for the next couple of days as almost all roads were blocked with big drifts. The storm ending also meant that the cold was coming, big-time cold with the absolute clearest sky imaginable.

About the third night I was sent with my sister to get milk. Getting ready meant sweatshirt and winter coats, a stocking cap, maybe insulated jeans, galoshes with buckles that allowed us to stuff our pants into the top and pull tight with the buckles and of course, two pairs of gloves. This time we wrapped scarves around our faces.

Stepping outdoors, freeing the sled from the snow, putting the box and my sister on the sled, we headed out. There was no street light on our street so it was totally dark out with only a hint of light coming from around the corner. At the school gymnasium we picked up our first street light and when we walked in front of the school the street light created a shadow. A dark and sharp shadow that grew and grew so that I became taller and taller. I attempted to jump across my shadow, which, as you imagine, cannot be done without a big imagination. The sled was easy to pull over the frozen road. I danced and pulled the sled with a little soft shoe, singing the 1915 version of "Me and My Shadow." Halfway down the block, another street light appeared and created shadows on both sides of us, one dying out while the other became brighter and brighter, but getting shorter and shorter. Rounding the corner, we lost the street lights but with a couple of blocks to go, house lights showed our way.

Just getting the money from my coat pocket to pay for the milk was a major job. Picking up the still warm milk, I put the jar into the box; then, with my sister holding the box and loaded back on the sled, the trip home was underway. With the milk now and the trip a little uphill required a slower return but I looked forward to the shadows with anticipation. On the way home the shadows seemed to mock, "Who knows what evil lurks in the hearts of men? The Shadow knows," followed by blood-curdling laughter. As we passed bushes and trees, the shadow might jump out. Oh, the fear of it all. By that time my sister was less than happy with me and, somewhat frightened, she might forget my swearing, so we hurried on home. I knew I would be in more trouble, but who could pass up the opportunity?

Arriving home, I was met with the demand to head right around to the back of the house and take care of the burn barrel. I protested that there was no light around back until I got a fire burning. But protesting did little good so I hurried to get the fire going to provide some needed heat, the kind that only warms one side at a time. Standing with one side soaking in the heat, I looked north and saw the brilliant array of the Northern Lights. The greens and blues rolled from the dark horizon and reached high into the sky. The lights were spectacular! As I turned around to warm my other side, looking to the mountains, the sky was ablaze with the most brilliant display of stars. I could pick out the faintest of stars, the Milky Way, and many constellations. The stars performed their own twinkling magic and then a shooting star crossed my line of vision. The darkness with the Northern Lights, the stars, and the shooting star and with only myself present made for a magic time. It was as if I were looking into the beginning of time and was the only one seeing it. I wondered if early man had felt this magic as he stood by his fire. The air was so clear and the cold was so intense. The feeling was broken when Mom called to me, "You want to catch your death by standing around in the cold?"

After an evening of listening to the radio, playing pinochle, cribbage or Hell with Mom or maybe working on a jigsaw puzzle, then off to bed. Hot water bottle, flannel sheets, and speed all helped make it bearable; I soon learned to never move from the spot where I started. Listening to the big power radio stations that boomed up from San Francisco and reading a book, mostly under the covers with no skin showing, I knew I was in for one more very special treat. During the night, Jack Frost would visit the windows around my bed, creating a very deep frost on the inside of the window. The patterns remained until the first rays of the sun struck the window and my bedroom area became a kaleidoscope of colors.

Party at Olsons

SINCE DAD WAS THE SUPERINTENDENT and high school principal in North Powder, he believed he needed to be careful in selecting close friends. Three families, besides ours, became close friends and were involved with each other in social events and activities. I was twelve and the other kids were close to the same age. When the event was held at the Olsons, we all went. Going to the Olsons was like traveling back in time. They lived far back in the country with a narrow dirt and gravel road that passed through a rock canyon to reach their homestead. The last part of the road went through a wheat field via a dirt lane. The house was a tall single-level house with clapboard sides that had weathered and darkened over many years. A broken-down picket fence surrounded the house and the outhouse. To the east, beyond the creek, were the barn and outbuildings. They were just as dried out as the home. Deer were everywhere. Close to the house, but outside the fence, was old farm equipment.

When we'd arrive, Bob and his wife greeted us as if we were long lost family. Bob was a tall string bean of a man. Esther was a short, round woman. They were ranchers and farmers who worked very hard on land that was marginal and in a climate, also marginal. Both she and Bob had that great anticipation for living and loving every minute of it.

We usually ate venison these nights, young venison with lots of gravy. Mom brought her scalloped potatoes and an angel food cake. Vivian and Bill, a part of the group, brought a salad of some sort and a chocolate cake with lots of thick chocolate frosting. Olive and Emory brought vegetables that had been home canned like green beans or creamed corn. While the food was brought into the kitchen, the men set up a bar on a buffet that ran along one side of a large room. A long table that seated fifteen to twenty people occupied most of the room, though it also had a wood stove, a piano, a few chairs, and some furniture moved back out of the way. There were only four other rooms: three smallish bedrooms and a kitchen. The kitchen had a large wood burning kitchen range with a hot water box on the side. The sink was on the other side of the kitchen opposite the range. A long flat sink with a small hand pump was connected directly to the well and provided very cold water. The hot water came from a large white-and-blue specked enameled pot with a bail handle and a pour spout that always sat on the range or dipped from the range tank. A long-slanted counter led into the sink.

While food preparation was going on the young people headed outside the house to the old equipment sitting there of a different era, the era of steam. We could do anything we wanted with this equipment as it had rusted and was frozen in time and place. So many levers, faucets, and dials, we wondered how it had all worked. There were a couple of tractors and a steam donkey with all types of farm equipment they might have pulled. With imagination, the farm and old equipment was a great place to visit. Of course, I did not live there or have to use it.

In winter, dinner was a little early as the cooking and dishes needed to be finished before dark. In the summer, it could be much later. When the federal government had set out to electrify the rural areas of the United States this ranch was beyond what they would do.

When the dinner bell rang we'd all gather around the table, sitting on chairs, benches, boxes, and barrels. We always had a happy and boisterous time. After dinner, the young people helped clear the table and then went back outside. Our parents all worked to get the dishes washed, dried, and put away. As dusk began to settle in this little valley the light of the kerosene lamps began to show through the windows and as we moved inside the pale rosy light from the lanterns gave a special glow to the room. The room was wall-papered with flickering shadows from people moving about. Then the table was moved out, chairs and seats were pushed against the wall. The room had a slick linoleum floor. Time to dance!

Vivian was the piano player. When she was a young lady she had played piano for local dance bands and she was good. She never had any music to read, but she knew all the songs that our parents loved. They were the songs of the war, big bands, honky-tonk, and any others that someone might know. The piano was an old upright with a rod in the upright portion that gave it a special tinny sound. It was magic!

Dancing was a must. Everyone danced, even Dad, though it was not what he enjoyed most. The kids were expected to dance with each other or with one of the moms. That room got very hot as the wood stove kicked out heat and bodies were flying around. Near the door, usually open, we might gather in some nice cool air. We could step outside for a short time to really cool off but we wouldn't linger; we were needed.

Later in the evening, as Vivian tired, she'd announce the last dance, and the party would wind down. The young people headed for different corners of the room to visit, talk about school, or even go to sleep. We knew to look for a comfortable place because the folks were settling in for cards, usually Canasta but it could be Pinochle. The games would go on and on, laughing and kidding along the way. Thinking back, they had such a great time.

If dark when we left, the ride home was surreal. Thousands of jack rabbits darted into the headlights of the car. There was a terrible infestation and we could not help but hear them as some never made it away from the car. Dad would swear, Mom would yell to watch out, and my sisters would cry in the back seat each time the car hit another one. I tried to keep track of the thumps or the bumps knowing another jack had gotten it. Every dead one meant it couldn't eat the crop the Olsons were trying to raise.

If starting to get light when it was time to go, we never left on an empty stomach. Breakfast was fixed for all. Bacon, scrambled eggs, hash browns with toast came out on big platters, all cooked on the large wood range. The toast was toasted on a four-sided toaster that sat over one of the burners where the lid had been removed. Dishes were done by all and then we went home to crash. In the spring, if we were very fortunate, we stopped at a lek, which is an area where the sage grouse strut and do their courting. Seeing the sage grouse was a very special treat.

The four couples remained close friends for a long time. Almost every month they would have a get-together. It went from family to family for many years. When we kids were in high school, we began to have other interests and usually did not attend. Times were tough, none of the families had much cash, but we sure knew how to have a good time together.

Huggin' and Chalkin'

THE SUMMER OF 1952 was the first real summer after leaving Arlington. Most of those summer days I was quite free to ride my bike on every single street in North Powder, which could be done in a short period of time as there were not many streets. What was special, with permission, I could ride out the Wolf Creek road where there were willow trees. Here I stopped to whittle a willow whistle. I made pretty good willow whistles and brought them back to my sisters.

Now to make a willow whistle you need a well-honed two-blade Case pocket knife. For the best whistle, you need a spring time straight piece of willow limb about the size of your pointing finger and twice as long. It needs to have at least three nodules. At the first nodule, you cut the mouth piece on a diagonal, locating the second nodule on the top. Just in front of the third nodule cut a line around the bark into the wood layer. Cut out the second nodule with a V. Then with the side of your Case, gently rap all the area from the mouth piece to the scribed line, all the time twisting the bark. It will break free and slide off. You need to keep that bark. On the bare stick, from the mouth piece to the V notch, slice off a small portion of the top. From and including the V notch whittle out a chamber toward the third notch. Slide the bark back in place and gently blow into the mouth piece; you should hear the whistle. Working with your

Case on the gap and the chamber will change the sound of the whistle. Any piece of the limb beyond the third nodule becomes an area of decoration. When the limb becomes dry, as they always will, you need to "wet your whistle."

The down side of the Wolf Creek road was that it was a gravel road but with my Schwinn's knee action, wide tire bike it made no difference to an expert rider. I made this ride often and noticed a couple of girls out in the yard of the Forest Service Compound. This compound had a house for the forester and his family. I did not know the girls, who looked to be a little younger than me. As I passed them we each waved as I continued on my way. Later in the day when I returned I would sometimes see them; if not, I'd just ride on home. One day I asked Mom about the girls; she said something about twins but that was about all.

A few days later I biked pass the Ranger Station. The twins were outside. We waved. I so wanted to stop and go over to visit but I did not have the nerve to do so. I kept on riding. When I reached my favorite willow whistle tree source I decided to make each of them a willow whistle that I would give to them when I returned home. If they were not outside, no way was I going to go to the door. I didn't even know their names. They were not outdoors so I took both of my sisters a whistle.

A day or two later I decided to try again. This time, just as I was finishing their whistles, I heard a clap of thunder. The race was on between me and the storm as to whether or not I was going to get soaked. I lost that race to lightning and thunder and the soaking rain. As I changed out of my soaking wet clothes, I realized I had become focused on meeting the two girls. Mom and Dad both reprimanded me for not keeping track of the weather.

The next time I started out was a Friday. I knew family friends were coming for dinner, which was great because

Billy was my best friend. This time as I rode out I did not see the girls but I was confident that I would on the way home. So I made the two best willow whistles ever and started back into town. As I approached the Forest Service compound, I saw that both girls were out front. *Perfect,* I thought. Being brave at heart I stopped, got off my bike, and walked it to the edge of the compound. They walked over and we began to visit. I presented them with my best ever willow whistles and they soon mastered the technique of blowing them. It seemed we were having a good time. We sat on logs lying in front of the compound, talking, and they blew their whistles. We talked about North Powder, other places we had lived, and about going to a new school.

Suddenly, their father stormed out of the office, came over to me, and told me to get off the property. Yelling that I was not to talk to the girls again! I ran to my bike, took off, and headed for home as quickly as possible. By the time I was home I was crying. I let my bike drop in the yard and ran on to the porch, my bedroom side. Mom tried her best to find out what was wrong and console me. It took some time before she got me squared away enough so I could talk coherently about the situation. She had no answers but she thought I would survive; besides Billy and his family were coming soon. I had to get my act together as I sure didn't want Billy to know I had been crying.

When Billy and his family arrived, he and I went out back and I told him of my experience of the day. I left out my crying, as it wasn't an important part of the story.

Billy asked, "Why didn't you stand up to the father?"

I said, "I'm sure you would have, ha! You would have done the same thing … RUN!"

He slugged my shoulder; I slugged him back. We went back inside and sat down with the folks to wait for dinner.

It wasn't long before my sisters came inside from the front yard. They said loudly, "You have two girls at the front door wanting to talk to you."

I was sure that everybody knew what had happened. The stillness in the house was like the world had stopped. I could hardly breathe. I went to the door with Billy at my side and saw the twins. I thought, *What are they doing here?*

One of the twins said they were sorry their father had yelled at me. He had mistaken me for someone else who had not been very nice to them, and that I should feel free to come visit anytime.

They thanked me for the whistles, I introduced them to Billy and my sisters, and off they went. A certain degree of confidence had been reestablished. I went back into the house, beaming and thinking that maybe they had stood up for me.

As I walked through the living room, I heard a deep voice. Billy's dad asked, "Have you been doing some 'huggin' and chalkin' that I didn't know about?"

"What do you mean, 'huggin' and chalkin'," I asked?

He replied, "You know, when you have a piece of chalk in your hand, you reach around the girl and give her a hug, drawing a line. The next time you reach a little farther and chalk another line. It looks like you need two pieces of chalk."

While everyone roared I could have melted into the floor.

The Reprieve

THREE OF MY CLASSMATES and I were riding to the garbage dump. We were riding our bikes to do some shooting, without parental guidance. We were in the eighth grade and were primed for adventure. Our single-shot 22s were over our handlebars. The rifles were not loaded but we had plenty of ammo in our pockets. What a great day it would be.

We rode along Highway 30, the major highway crossing Oregon; this was all before the Interstate. We faced a three- or four-mile journey on the road from North Powder to Union. We knew we would be passed by the traffic traveling Highway 30, but it wouldn't be a problem as we had made the ride many times picking up stubby beer bottles for two cents apiece. Being a Saturday and in the fall, the traffic should be light.

Our first hill was a moderate climb out of North Powder, which I was used to as part of my paper route. Fall rides are very pleasant, warm but not hot, aromas of many kind such as the gypo saw mill, smoke from people burning leaves, the whirl of the saws cutting slab wood, and the smell of new, second cut hay would be part of our day. As we left town we picked up speed on a long downhill stretch. We were moving, but in a line, as the road was not wide. We were all being careful.

We passed the Marie Dorian sign, which was a history roadside sign. Marie Dorian was an Indian woman who had the first mixed race child born in the Oregon country. The child was born just outside of North Powder, but we all knew this and kept right on peddling our one speed bikes. We entered the willows, an area along the highway in which willow trees had been planted. These great willow trees offered shade along the way of our trek. In the spring, they had been especially important as a source of willow sticks, which made excellent willow whistles. They grew quickly and were conveniently placed along the highway. In this area, the water table was high and encouraged growth that almost created a canopy of cover.

Going through this flat land, we usually had a breeze or wind in our faces, which made riding a little harder, but that did not matter. We were passed by a number of travelers who must have thought it very strange to see four young boys riding bikes with rifles over the handlebars. We finally reached the road to the dump and as it was gravel and up a fairly steep hill, it soon required pushing our bikes. Finally, we made it.

The garbage dump was full of different kinds of garbage area. Everyone brought their own barrels with the rotting type of household garbage. This area we stayed away from! Then there was the old car area, the bottle area, old appliance area, the old bed frame area, all of which we needed because it was now time to load and shoot. We started with bottles on frames, a regular shooting gallery, working to be as successful breaking bottles farther and farther away. We then moved to more difficult shots involving parts of old car windows, tail lights that had not yet been broken out or any other unique spot that counted as a target. Then, we moved to the edge of the household garbage area where the rats were located. We spotted many rats and fired away. We were never sure just how many rats we killed as we thought some must have been wounded; they were dead in our sights, but disappeared in the garbage.

As we got low on ammunition, we became a little more selective in our targets. We turned around and to our startled eyes a small forked-horn buck was watching us, heaving, its legs kind of spread out as if it had been running for quite some time. We debated if this was a target meant just for us. We were not even sure if our 22 shells would penetrate the hide. We decided to shoot and we all did!

We knew almost immediately that we had done something we should not have done. The young buck went down, like a rock. We knew this was not good. We walked up to the buck and addressed the problem. We didn't see any blood and nudged it with our toes, but it did not move. We debated what we were going to do. We had hunted enough with our families to know that we could not leave it where it was; we had to take care of it, in a proper hunting way. None of us had a knife or admitted to having a knife, so the debate began. We decided to take it to one of the outbuildings on one of our friends' ranch that generally was not used. Then we could get a knife and do the appropriate hunting cleaning rituals. To get it there we decided to attach a leg to each of our handle bars and every one of us would have a leg.

We needed wire, and since we were in a dump, it was easy to find. We set up the bikes, two by two, brought the deer in between and began wiring up each leg. We had to set the bikes farther apart as the head was still resting on the ground. We got on our bikes and began moving down the gravel road, still carrying our rifles. The gravel road did not help; we found ourselves moving away and back together as we hit rocks and debris. The deer's head kept getting caught and would then spring forward. We had not gone far and realized this was going to be a very difficult job. We stopped and pondered the situation as only eight grades can ponder. We decided it would be easier as we got on the pavement, but then wondered about the cars and maybe even a policeman driving by and then jail was all but certain. We discussed turning the buck around so that only the head would drag, but we decided to go on without making the switch. We moved down the hill toward the highway when suddenly we noticed some life in our young buck. It was squealing and began to kick its legs. It got squirrely on the bikes and we all yelled and tried to stop, though a steep hill, gravel roads, and stopping do not necessarily go together. We dragged our feet when one of the deer's legs broke free and it really began moving. Now was time to leave our bikes any way we could. The four bikes headed to the side, we went the other direction, the deer kicked more and suddenly free of any encumberment, off it went. So much for our wiring job. We realized we were relieved of the outcome and needed to have another ponder session.

We stopped to discuss what had happened. Then we wondered why the deer did not thank us for the ride. He was probably the only deer that saw the world from an upside-down position and what would he ever tell the herd. The four of us decided right there and then that no one would ever tell the story to anyone. Can you imagine the laughing stock we would become? The four of us never talked about it again.

I may be the only one left to tell the story. The story needed to be told.

Catfish and Frog Legs

"BILLY AND BOBBY, I want you to stay after school," said Mr. Irons, our seventh grade teacher.

Billy and I looked at each other and carried on a conversation by motion.

What did we do? Billy asked with his hands.

I shrugged back, *I didn't do anything.*

We both knew if we were in trouble at school we were in serious trouble at home. Mr. Irons was my next-door neighbor. Not only was my dad the superintendent and principal, but Bill's dad was chairman of the School Board. We were really concerned about what we had done. We had no idea what had gotten us into trouble and kept shaking our heads and shrugging our shoulders. The rest of the class kept looking at us, nodding their heads with a little smirk. Finally, the bell rang; it was time to go for all except the two of us. We just sat in our seats.

After they left, Mr. Irons sternly told us to come up to his desk and then let us stand there. "Scared you a bit, didn't I?" he chuckled.

"Mr. Irons, that is not funny," I said and Billy quickly agreed. "You scared us a lot."

"How would you like to go catfishing in Union tomorrow?"

"Tomorrow?" we both answered. Looking at each other, we quickly nodded yes.

"You need to be ready to go at 5:30 sharp! Make sure you have gear, worms, jacket, and a lunch."

Billy and I had been badgering Mr. Irons to take us catfishing. He had grown up in Union, our neighboring town, had always fished, and knew the best places to fish. He always had an excuse for not taking us but now it looked like we were in. What a great time we would have. We didn't even ask for permission as we both knew it would be given. We had to get everything we needed ready in just a couple of hours before dark. Frantic digging for worms, gear all ready with extra wine cork bobbers, lunch made in the evening as 5:30 a.m. was coming soon.

We would be fishing for Bullhead catfish. When Dad and I fished for bullheads we went in the evening. We started a fire near the edge of the pond or along the edge of a slough. I would fasten a cork or if I could afford it, a bobber to my line, allowing the worm on the hook to dangle in the water close to the bottom. We would cast out the weighted hook and worm. I would reel the line back in so it tightened, put my rod in a forked stick shoved into the pond edge so the tip was up and the handle, held to the ground with a rock. The light of the fire was to attract the catfish to the area.

The fire needed to burn for many hours. The best way to keep the fire going was to throw on an old tire or two. Looking back, I am sure the smoke was toxic and I smelled like rubber smoke for days, but the fire kept me warm and the mosquitoes at bay. When the cork or bobber disappeared, I would run up, grab my pole, set the hook, and start reeling the catfish in. They were caught ... hook, line, and sinker. I would bring the fish ashore and then we needed to disengage the hook. Here was a problem; the catfish had sharp barbs for whiskers and I wanted to avoid getting zapped. It only took one zap to realize I did not want another. It hurt! But after freeing the fish, it went into the gunny sack, kept in the water, waiting to be taken home. There was no limit or rather, the limit was the number of fish we wanted to skin and fillet.

So, in the spring of 1952 Billy and I were riding with Mr. Irons, heading to the Union ponds. To us, this was an earth-shaking event. We were actually going the find his secret ponds to fish. Of course, he made us pledge to never tell anyone else. And fish we did! We caught so many fish and didn't smell like burnt rubber fire. Between the three of us, one always had a fish on, sometimes two had fish on, and a few times all three had a fish on. What a morning!

We nearly had a gunny sack full and were getting ready to head to the car when very innocently, Mr. Irons asked, "Have you ever fished for frogs?"

"Frogs, frogs," Billy and I replied in unison. "No, but we are ready. But what are we going to do with frogs?" I asked.

Mr. Irons questioned, "You've never eaten frog legs?" He had baited the hook and we were caught. We were going for frogs; we just did not understand our role in procuring them. We were back at the car to drop off the gunny sack of catfish.

Mr. Irons had planned this from the beginning, I could see, as he got a long pole out of the car. He attached a large treble hook with some line. Then he said, "This is illegal."

"What is?" Billy asked. We didn't get an answer.

"Come on!" he said as he stepped through the barb wire fence. Billy and I looked at each other and started running after him. Mr. Irons listened for a bull frog and began working toward it, motioning us to stay right where we were. He cast over the bull frog and drew the line back, hoping to snag it. The second or third time he successfully snagged the frog. The frog went berserk; it did not want to be caught but Mr. Irons prevailed. Billy and I were laughing so hard over the antics of the frog and Mr. Irons. We then found out our role in this adventure. We were to hold the big bull frog while he went after another with the instructions, "Do not let the frog loose."

That bull frog and the three others he caught did not want to be held. We knew our place in school demanded that we not lose one. We survived by holding them by the back legs, one in each hand. One of us volunteered to go get another gunny sack but Mr. Irons was sure he did not have another. We kept asking if it wasn't about time to go and he kept responding, "Just one more cast." The first one was caught quickly; the last three seemed to take forever. Finally, we went back to the car and by darn, he had another sack. He knew it all the time! He wanted us to hold those kicking, squirming, jumping frogs.

What a day, fishing and frogging. We were tired and could hardly wait to get home to take a well-deserved nap. We both fell asleep on the way home and woke up in front of Mr. Irons' home.

"Well, boys," he said, "to victors come the spoils and all these catfish and frogs need to be killed and cleaned." We both groaned. His wife, Betty, must have loved us coming into the kitchen with two gunny sacks. I'm sure we made quite a mess. The bull frogs were taken out one at a time, killed and the legs severed from the body and skinned. The catfish, still alive but not very frisky, were dumped into the sink, then grabbed, and their heads were pushed onto a nail sticking through a board. They were skinned and filleted. Billy and I had so many fish to clean, our parents came over to watch the show. Mr. Irons was laughing so hard trying to tell of the day's activities, while Billy and I kept working on the fish.

I asked Billy, "How many fish do you think we had in this gunny sack?"

He responded, "Way too many. I tell you, way too many."

Then I asked, "How many fish did Mr. Irons clean?"

"Just one or two to show us how to do it," he replied, but neither of us complained.

Early in the evening Mr. Irons began cooking the frog legs and the fillets. The frog legs kept jumping around in the pan. He didn't even have to turn them over; they jumped themselves. We tasted the frog legs, which were good, but they did kind of taste like chicken. The catfish fillets were breaded and fried in bacon grease and were they ever delicious. All the families sat and ate little fillets, though Billy and I never got very many to eat. We were too tired and we just wanted to sleep.

In class on Monday, Mr. Irons told the whole story to the uproarious laughter of our fellow students. Of course he included some exaggerations, especially about holding onto the frogs. He had more fun at our expense telling the story. We were kidded about this fishing trip for quite some time. We had learned, however; neither one of us ever, ever again asked Mr. Irons to take us catfishing.

Halloween

THE GET-TOGETHER AT OUR HOUSE that Halloween eve in 1952 was about to end. Billy, Steve, Jimmy, Mary Lou, and I — all classmates who lived in town — had been regaled with stories by Billy's dad, who had grown up in North Powder and knew all the famous Halloween Eve pranks. Like the buckboard ending up on top of the Hudelson Mercantile building where it sat for years because no one knew how to safely remove it from the roof. And the outhouse lassoed by a couple of local cowboys while a friend had fallen asleep inside protecting it. The two cowboys then dragged it to the nearby North Powder river and set it afloat, though they did rescue the friend when it floated under the bridge. Being very grateful, the now wide-awake rescued one bought the rescuers beers, all the time threatening to shoot whoever had pulled this prank on him. And the time some cowboys brought a young steer to town, where they proceeded to kill it, hang it, and dress it out in the entrance of the U.S Post Office. The sauce of the thirteen saloons then located in North Powder might have been a factor. But they were great stories that fired our imagination and thirst for fame.

At the house by the light of a single candle, we each read aloud some Edgar Allen Poe, just to put a little darkness into the night. We also began talking about how to achieve fame for a great prank that might become part of the lore of

Halloween in North Powder. We did not have an answer but we were ready to go! Our first stop would be at Mrs. Lund's. It was only a couple of houses away but we knew she made the best popcorn balls in town and we each needed one to munch on as we worked our way to the center of town. As we walked and talked we knew we were through with the old 'nail, notched wooden spool, and string mischief' that created a crashing sound on the window, we had not planned ahead for the cow pile in a paper sack to set afire on the porch, and the soaping of windows was too passé for our little group of 'townies.'

We knew that Mr. and Mrs. Craig were handing out full-size candy bars, but we saved that for later, so we decided to 'trick or treat' one of the remaining three bars to see if we might get candy. The five of us went into the Wheel, the largest of the bars. Someone there announced our arrival and said he was buying, but first we all had to have a chew from a plug of tobacco. Sure, we could handle the situation. All but Mary Lou said, "Yes, we do it all the time." Like fools we pulled a chew from the plug, the most vile, gross thing we had ever tasted. We soon got out of the bar, spitting out the yuck, feeling queasy and without our candy bars. We heard the laughter as the door shut behind us. That taste remained with us for most of the night, no matter what treats we found.

We then began looking seriously as to what shenanigans we should try. We finally decided, for lack of a better idea, to tip over an outhouse or two. In North Powder there were many outhouses, most of them no longer being used as indoor bathrooms and septic fields were added to houses. Steve's foot slipped while we pushed one; it got a little gross. While the rest of us roared, even Steve laughed. We found a spigot with water that had not yet been turned off and he washed most of it off with very little help from us. It convinced us that our time for tipping outhouses was over and a certain amount of fame was not coming our way.

We had walked most of the town, too old for treats, too young for the big tricks. We decided to take one more pass through of the heart of downtown. We noticed that someone had moved and stacked the sheriff's wood pile from along his garage to across the street. We wished we had thought of that or had even helped, but we could take no credit. As we neared downtown we heard the voices of older kids and decided to check it out. They had started what became known as the "Schima War."

The Schimas lived in a house next to the Hudelsons' Mercantile Store and just below the Hudelsons' home and sloping vacant lot. The Schimas' house was not very large — just right for a couple and two boys — but it had a very nice, large, four-holer outhouse. I never knew why they had a four-holer. Can you imagine a family sitting together, like a family that contemplates together or solves problems together? We quickly learned that almost every year the outhouse became the target of the juniors and seniors and even some graduates who might still be around to do a tip over. Every year Mr. Schima wrapped his outhouse with chicken wire and applied electricity. He defiantly defended his outhouse, but the kids on the hill were just as determined. Someone threw a rock and sparks flew in all directions as the rock hit the chicken wire. The five of us 'townies' were told to find rocks for the older ones to throw. It was heating up! We were now included.

Mr. Hudelson had a few old military surplus trucks sitting on the highest portion of the vacant lot. The tires were flat. They had not been moved for years. But with enough people pushing, one truck started to move. Being open-cabbed, someone jumped in to steer. The truck moved, slowly, ever so slowly. Pointed in the direction of the outhouse, it picked up speed. The one steering jumped free as momentum carried the truck down the slope straight toward the Schima outhouse. Mr. Schima saw the truck barreling down the slope and yelled, "No! no! no!" and jumped back into the house. The truck was locked in as if on a military guidance system. What a perfect hit. The truck crashed into the outhouse with enough force to break it up into kindling, with sparks flying in all directions. When the cheer went up from the crowd that had gathered, we knew we had been part of something great, the 'Schima War.'

Our story just might join the other great Halloween tricks.

Haying for the Davis'

"BOBBY! BOBBY! What did you do to my tractor?" asked Bill, Billy's dad.

Timidly I asked, "What do you mean?" as he headed over to the right side of the tractor and looked at the bunch rake attached to it.

"I thought so." He pointed to the right end of the rake and said, "It's bent; you hit a fence post on the drive out to the field. I have told you and reminded you that your rake is wider than the tractor and you have to watch out how close you get to things beyond the edge of the tractor. Well, let me see if it has to be repaired." He climbed on to test and operate the rake. "It's bent but not enough to cause any damage. You don't think I have enough to do around here that I want to spend haying time putting in a new fence pole?"

How could I be so careless or not feel it hit, I wondered. "I will stay late to fix it."

"No" he replied, "You wouldn't know how."

I notice that the fence post was not repaired during the season and every time I drove by I saw wires hanging loose. Was that missing wooden fence post a reminder to be more careful?

On a Friday spring day, 1954. Billy and I were riding our

bikes after school, heading to his family ranch on the edge of North Powder. The day was very special: warm and sunny, with the feeling of spring having finally arrived in the valley. We could hear the meadowlarks as we left the school. It had been a long, cold winter. We rode slowly and visited with DeEtte, Karen, and Helen as they walked home. They were younger but none of the girls in our class walked home. Billy and I regaled them with the greatness of our being freshmen and how they needed to watch out for their freshmen initiation next year.

I did not stay with Billy overnight as I had papers to deliver in the morning but I helped him with his chores in the evening. He had lots of chores: getting the wood in, chopping kindling, taking care of his 4-H calf, feeding barn animals, slopping the hogs, milking two or three cows, separating the milk, cleaning the separator, and maybe even riding out into the field in the beat-up old 30s red International pickup to check a fence line. I didn't mind helping with all his chores except the milking; I could never get the hang of it or rather the squeeze-and-pull of it. In the morning he had to do all these chores again plus he might have to go out in the field to feed the cattle with the hay that had been put up the previous summer.

In the evening, before I left for home, Billy's dad offered me a haying job in the coming hay season, mid-summer. I was quick to respond with a "yes." Billy and I thought it was a great idea to be working together. The chance to spend time with my best friend sounded good, never mind the fact I got hay fever, big time. One requirement of Bill's was that Billy had to make sure I knew how to drive and care for the Ferguson. That meant practice! The Ferguson drove much like a car with a stick shift, five speeds forward and a clutch to shift. The throttle was a lever on the steering wheel shaft that sat in the center between the large rear wheels. Two smaller wheels were in front, spaced the same as the rear wheels. I had to learn to grease, check the oil, clean the radiator, check fluids, the whole nine yards. I thought it was perfect!

The Davises raised their hay to feed their cattle over the winter and spring. Most of this hay was raised on very prime grass and alfalfa growing land. Although hay bailers were coming into use in Eastern Oregon, the Davis's used the loose hay stack type of preserving their feed as they would be feeding the cattle from the stack.

The time came to start using my new skills. Billy and the hired hand, Ed, had started mowing one of the fields a couple of days before I started to work. One was driving a Farmall tractor while the other drove a John Deere. Both had narrow fronts with two small tires, wide and tall large rear tires, and the driver sat elevated. Billy and Ed were both operating a sickle bar mower that sat behind them on a platform. When lowered, the sickle bar traveled back and forth rapidly, parallel to the ground, cutting the hay between the teeth. The mower slid along the ground conforming to the grounds contour. It could stand upright, like a semaphore, when not mowing if the tractor needed to be moved. Every day they needed to check the sickle bar for damaged, loose, or lost teeth and replace them. Every day they needed to grease all the moving parts. This mowing left the hay lying on the ground, drying.

Depending on the heat and dryness of the air, I used a side delivery rake to put the dry hay into windrows. I reported to work and Bill put me to the test. I would be using the Ferguson and towing the rake behind. First, I had to show him I knew how to care for the tractor. Billy had taught me well. I passed with a pat on the back with a, "Let's hook up the rake." I drove around the pasture towing the rake. It had two larger wheels off set and at an angle; as the tractor pulled the rake forward the tines of the fork rolled the hay to the left. It had two crazy wheels that balanced the rake and let it go in any direction. Bill followed as I towed it to the field. At the field, Bill told me that for the first row I would move the rake from right to left, bringing the hay away from the fence row into the field. At corners, I would do a tight loop which would help me get all the hay from the corner. My next trip around the field would be in the opposite direction, creating a double piled windrow. At each completion of the trip around the field I would turn to the other direction. After a lap or two, Bill said, "I think you got it, be careful and we will see you later in the day."

At noon Billy and Ed came over and we had lunch and then a short time later we were back at work. They moved to another field to mow and I was back raking the one I started. I was beginning to really suffer with hay fever. I had put a bandana around my face but I was still suffering. I tried to wash my face but that had little effect. I remained about two days behind. When we quit for the evening my rake was left in the field and I drove the tractor back to the house. I could hardly see; my hay fever was so bad my eyes were almost swollen shut. Bill asked me if I was going to survive and he understood if I had to quit.

"No way, I will be back tomorrow." When home, Dad took me over to the gym locker room and had me use the locker room shower as we only had a bathtub. One of the perks of having Dad the superintendent.

Next morning, I was loaded up with Dristan, ready to tackle the new day and I survived, though I always had a couple of farmer-sized handkerchiefs to use, which, by the end of the day were completely soaked. A couple of days into the raking, the first field was windrowed. Leaving the side-deliver rake in the field I went back to the barn. Bill and I attached the bunch trip rake, which was used to create large bunches of hay out of the windrows. When I finished a windrow there would be, along the same line, a number of bunches. A couple of days later I clipped the fence.

Billy and Ed each drove a hay buck. The hay buck was fabricated from an old car. The transmission, steering wheels and seat were reversed so that the turning wheels were now in back and the drive wheels were in front. This allowed the heat of the engine and exhaust to be kept away from the dry hay, removing some fire danger. The new front now had a bar with teeth that slid along the ground. The bar could be lifted hudraulically a few inches so they could move swiftly around the field without catching one of the teeth in the ground. The teeth were straight, seven-foot long raw sawed pine spars, pointed at the front to slide along the ground. Ten spars or teeth were fitted on the bar. They hay bucker would gather a number of bunches and take them to where they hay stack was to be built.

Billy remembered when a large, three-legged derrick with a lifting arm sat in the field. It had been used to lift and stack the hay, and horses provided the power to lift. But in 1954 Bill had a hydraulic lift fork on the Farmall tractor that did that work. As the larger bunches were moved closer to the stack, Ed placed the now larger bunches onto the stack under the direction of Billy's dad, who was on top of the stack, directing and moving the hay to just where he wanted it. He was a master stack builder, building the stack so it would shed the water when it rained or the snow melted. The outer layer of hay operated much like the thatch roof houses of England, keeping the hay dry and usable. Bill also stressed the shape, compactness and to always remember the number one rule of hay stacking: "Keep the tines pointing down when you lean the pitch fork into the stack." You never wanted to find yourself sliding off the stack onto the pitch fork.

125

After the stack was finished, board fences surrounded the stack to keep the deer and cattle from feeding from it. This process was used for the rest of the fields and later for a second cutting or, if fall weather held, they might get a small third cutting. This hay was now ready for the winter of 1954 and spring of 1955. When this hay was used, the lift fork was used again, this time to load the hay wagon. The hay was pitch-forked off of the wagon as it moved around the field to feed the cattle.

But my haying career was at an end. I had suffered tremendously for the first and second cuttings. Billy and I had not gotten to work together as we had hoped but I felt I had helped Billy's family. I had gotten a taste of farm work and would have enjoyed it if I could have survived the hay fever. I ended up with a few dollars in my pocket and a great deal of experience. I got a kick out of driving the tractor and taking care of it.

Sometime later I was with Billy in the old pickup and went by my wooden fence post. It had been replaced.

Rattlesnake Canyon

"LET'S GO FISHING," I yelled at LeRoy as I rode my bike back from the post office on a chore from Dad.

"When?" he asked.

"Just as soon as I can put a few worms in the Prince Albert can and make a peanut butter sandwich. At the post office in thirty minutes." A couple of minutes later I saw Jimmy. "Join LeRoy an' me and let's go fishing."

"Sure" he said.

"Meet at the post office in thirty minutes." I hurried on home. Running in the house, I told Mom, "LeRoy and Jimmy are going fishing; is it okay if I go?" Not waiting for a reply, "I need a peanut butter sandwich and some worms."

"Well, you know where the bread and peanut butter are and I do not do worms." She kind of laughed but I had received my permission to go. My sister, Lynne, piped up about going.

"No way, this is for older guys who can ride their bikes a long way and are able to deal with rattlesnakes."

Lynne said, "I don't want to go if you see snakes."

"Young man, you're not going if you are going to Rattlesnake Canyon."

"No, Mom, we are not going to Rattlesnake Canyon and yes we will see snakes, but they will be garter snakes."

"Well, you better hurry," Mom said as I ran out the door with a sandwich. I quickly grabbed some worms from our worm tub. I stopped long enough to fill from the garden hose my real, World War II military surplus canteen with a snap cover on a real web military belt. I put the belt on, worms in my back pocket, sandwich in a small knap sack with a few extra hooks and split shot, and grabbing my pole, pushed off with all the gear, swinging my leg over the rear wheel, and I was gone. I heard Mom yell, "What time will you be back?"

"Before dinner." I looked back at Mom and my sisters, and added, "Would one of you please take the mail to Dad?"

I knew I was late, about half an hour, but expected LeRoy and Jimmy to be late, too, which they were. We were heading to the North Powder River, which drained the northwest end of Baker Valley, a short ride down to the train depot where we would leave our bikes, then walk about a quarter of a mile to the river. When we did this jaunt in the spring and early summer, we would fish for trout. In late summer, we were fishing for suckers, big suckers! Suckers were a trash fish not suitable for eating. Many of the ones we caught would reach twenty inches or longer.

The North Powder River was used extensively for irrigation. Irrigation water taken out and the low summer flow of water created a series of connecting long ponds. As we approached the river we crouched down, hiding behind the brush that lined the bank of the river. The fish were very skittish and seeing us or our shadows would scare them and they would not bite. Eventually we crawled down that last little bit, turned to sit up, bait the hook, cast out and wait. We knew from experience that we were only going to get one shot at a sucker in that hole. If a small one took the bait, that was it, no big one for us this time. The three of us started at a different hole and then leap-frogged over each other on our way down the river. In really hot weather we had fun just wading down the river stopping at the riffles to fish the hole ahead and never get out of the river.

LeRoy always caught the biggest and the most fish. We were always amazed how many he caught. Jimmy and I caught our share but nothing like LeRoy. We used an early type of catch and release system. All the suckers caught were thrown up on the bank. The carcasses became the spoil for the scavengers. The scavengers might be raptors, crows, magpies, coyotes, or even a badger. At one time or another we had seen them working on the carcasses. Along the way we stopped for lunch, usually under some big willow trees that lined the bank. We all agreed we should have packed a larger lunch.

As the afternoon wore on we began to think about when and where we were going to head back to our bikes. Part of the decision rested on how fishing had been and if we still had worms. This time we did. We had to make a decision. We could fish back up the river for by now the earlier holes would be calm and we would catch more suckers. This was not our favorite approach as it took longer. The second choice was to cut though the Davis ranch. Billy and his family were good friends and would not mind if we went through the gates if we made sure we closed them. They did not want us climbing over barb wire fences as that tended to pull the wire from the wooden posts. Sometimes the gates were not very convenient, which made for a long detour. The Davises were cattle ranchers and we were very leery in which fields the bulls were located. The bulls and us in the same field did not sound good.

Our third choice was to continue down the river to where the North Powder River joined the Powder River. Then we could get on the Union Pacific Railroad track and walk the track back to North Powder. That point was also where the tracks came out of Rattlesnake Canyon, which was really the top of Telocaset Grade, but we knew it only as Rattlesnake Canyon. It had been drummed into us that we were not to go in the canyon, there were too many rattlers, too dangerous. During the day, all three of us had all been startled with a garter snake as we climbed up the bank of the river. It seemed to be looking at us at eye level. I am sure it startled the snake and I know it startled a young boy. So, we were leery and during lunch we discussed whether the rattlers would know if they were out of the canyon. I knew I had seen them when I was working in the hay fields for the Davises but maybe they were not canyon rattlers. We were alert for any odd motion.

Our fourth option, the one we were going to use, was to stop where we were, head across Davis's land, straight to the railroad tracks. The only real problem with this plan was some marsh land before the tracks and a very tight barbed wire fence that lined the railroad. Since we had been in the water and we were already muddy, we headed home that way. Working together, we climbed the fence with just a few grabs by the barbs and after reaching the tracks, an easy walk to our bikes. Track walking gave us time to practice walking the rails. Sometimes a train went by but the whistle blew long before it got to us, giving us plenty of time to clear the tracks.

Getting to our bikes, it was a quick ride home just in time for me to ask, "What's for dinner? I'm starving!"

"Well, no dinner for you until you stop right where you are, turn around, and head outside. I have to hose you off!"

"Oh, Mom."

"And put those worms back into the tub!"

"Well, what are we having for dinner?" I asked again.

"Baked spam," Mom replied.

Radio and TV

"THIS IS RADIO KBKR in Baker, Oregon, reducing power as required by the FCC. It is now sunset." That message ended my day listening to the only station I could receive on my small kit radio I had purchased and assembled. The radio was a round cylinder that I wrapped with wire with a rod passing along the cylinder that tuned in the station. I listened to a tinny sounding speaker. It was battery powered with alligator clips attached to a wire that ran from the radio to a 6-inch high, 3-inch in diameter battery. I used this radio sparingly; the batteries were expensive.

A couple of months later, the message was the same:

"This is radio KBKR in Baker, Oregon, reducing power as required by the FCC. It is now sunset." That message ended my day listening to the only station I could receive on my Tandy radio that I ordered out of a catalog of ready-to-assemble radio kits. Not much larger than my first radio, it had a dial, a couple of tubes, a little larger speaker and it plugged in. No more batteries. It even needed a soldering iron to put it together. There was still only the one local station, but it had an antenna that I stretched around my bedroom. At night, I could now listen to the power stations from San Francisco, Portland, and Seattle as they powered up at sunset.

Listening to the radio had always been important to my

family and me. As we kids lay on the floor in front of the fan of our Ziegler central oil heater, we listened on a large Magnavox console cabinet radio. Mom and Dad sat in easy chairs listening and reading books. I was often reading comic books or doing homework while we listened to *The Whistler* and whistled along with him or cackled with *The Shadow* when he asked, "Who knows what evil lies in the heart of man; the Shadow knows," or charged around the room to the sound of the William Tell Overture and to the hoof beats of the Lone Ranger and his faithful Indian friend, Tonto. Or perhaps we answered the phone for "Duffy's Tavern, Duff speaking," or swear I could almost smell the smoke of *Gunsmoke.*

In 1953, as a gift from Santa, I received a bedside Zenith radio, a white Bakelite plastic, maybe a foot wide and eight inches high with golden knobs and dials. Its antenna was coiled and fastened inside on the back. When I turned it on, light escaped along the edge of the back and I soon felt heat emanating from the back and the top. The heat was good as I knew the tubes in the radio were working. If the radio stayed cool I needed to replace the burned-out tube. I tested the tubes at a tester kiosk at the grocery store and hoped they still had the one I needed. At night, in bed, covers over my head, face out from the covers for light and reading a book, I would listen to the big power stations of San Francisco, Portland, and Seattle. I could now listen to the Oregon State Beavers and the recreated broadcast of the Portland Beavers baseball team.

The most important late-night radio programs were *Shakey's Pizza Parlor Request Hour* and *Lucky Lager Dance Time*. On the request hour, young people requested and listened to what was new in music while they ate pizza. My friends and I didn't even know what pizza was. None of my classmates had ever had pizza, but it must be good. As Saturday night evening lengthened into the wee hours of the morning, I listened to *Lucky Lager Dance Time*. The program beamed in from Seattle. The music was so cool and in my mind, I danced with April all that I wanted. Maybe I danced with one or two others, but the last dance was always with April as the show closed with, "I'll See You in My Dreams."

The fall of 1956 was important at our house. Dad purchased a TV in time to watch the 1956 World Series between the New York Yankees and the Brooklyn Dodgers. It turned out to be one of the greatest World Series ever and we watched it! The Yankees won the series in seven games. We watched Don Larson pitch his perfect game. Many of our teachers had the game on the radio during class. We knew what was happening so a couple of my classmates and I slipped over to my house, which was across the street, and watched it in black and white. We knew we were not going to be in too much trouble as Dad was already home watching the game.

But to say we watched it was arguable. We received a weak signal from Boise, Idaho. We had two antennas as there were two Boise stations and we were on the very fringe of their signal. One antenna was attached to a flat spot on the top of the roof. It had a thirty-foot mast with guy wires to the corner of the house. It took three people to set the optimum direction for best reception. One person stood on the flat spot of the roof, ready to turn the pole, yelling down to the person on the ground who talked to the person sitting in front of the TV. The person inside watched and told the window person whether the pole should be turned to the right or left. The other station and the other antenna was on a separate pole woven through the branches of a tree. It ended up pointing about 90 degrees from the first antenna. Its signal was much weaker than the first and all seemed to believe it was aimed at a metal barn so we were catching a bounced signal. Of course, both poles we grounded for lightning.

We suddenly had joined the world and there we were, watching the World Series from New York! It is true that sometimes we needed to go outside the house and look through a window at the TV screen which, for some reason, removed some of the 'snow.' Sometimes the 'snow' was so bad on the screen we only listened to the program or the event. Every so often I went up on the roof or up in the tree trying to 'tweak' the picture a bit. Always trying to improve the picture, Dad would purchase the next great antenna and back up the roof I went. For the first time, friends and I could watch *American Bandstand* with Dick Clark after school. In the evening friends would come over and watch *The Ed Sullivan Show*, *The $64,000 Question,* or *Gunsmoke*. Our life was beginning to change as we began to see this new world.

But when I went to bed, I still slipped under the covers, turned on the light to read, turned on the music to listen to *Shakey's Pizza Parlor Request Hour* and *Lucky Lager Dance Time* and dance the last dance with April in my dreams. So some things had not changed.

The Cider Jug Jamboree

"MORE APPLES," I yelled. "More apples; we need more apples."

Sharon yelled back, "How about these banana apples?"

Yelling back, "What do you mean, banana apples?"

She said, "These apples from the tree along the fence from the deserted farm that were yellow and tasted just like bananas."

"Throw them in! They will just mix with all the other apples."

Then Billy asked, "What about these that have worm hole bad spots?"

"Throw them in! We need more cider."

The Cider Jug Jamboree was the school carnival for Powder Valley High School. Its purpose was for the high school classes to raise money for various class activities. It also paid for touring activities such as National School Assemblies. The carnival happened in the gymnasium on a Friday night in early October. A large tarp covered the floor and booths were erected to handle the various carnival activities. The activities were for all levels: a fish pond for the youngest, dart toss, ping pong toss for goldfish, drive-a-nail, basketball shoot, Go-to-jail, B-B gun shoot, cake walk, and bingo, just to name a few.

The Jamboree required the help of all high school kids and teachers. The cider and the cookies that were sold with the cider were the biggest money maker and were given to the junior class. The junior Home Ec. girls made cookies for weeks. The juniors had the expense of the Junior-Senior Prom and Banquet. The senior class took care of the bingo and the cake walk. They had the Senior Dance and other graduating expenses. Prizes for bingo came from the business community in Baker and La Grande. A pair of senior students would go to each retail business and ask for donated items. We were very seldom turned down. The cakes came from the mothers; the mothers were out to demonstrate their ability. Freshmen and sophomores manned the carnival booths in which the prizes were awarded.

I was the junior class president and the class was making apple cider, lots of apple cider. We had the responsibility to make apple cider for the Cider Jug Jamboree coming up in two weeks. The day was Saturday, a beautiful fall day, crisp in the morning and heating up during the day. The entire class had gathered, all thirteen of us. Previously, we had gone out in the fields around North Powder where we located trees with available apples. Now we were back to pick the apples. Some of the trees were on deserted farms. We backed a pickup under the tree so we could shake the apples — worms, bruises and all — right into the pickup bed. We moved from tree to tree getting more apples. It didn't matter what variety of apple; we just needed apples, two pickup loads.

The pickup loads went to Emil Miller's farm where we had arranged to use his cider press. We backed up one of the pickups and started to work. Previously we had gathered containers to hold the cider. We started out straining the cider, taking out most of the flotsam and jetsam. That didn't last too long; we thought maybe we could skim it off later. We had lots of cider to press.

Emil Miller had a gas station in North Powder that sold treats like cokes, ice cream, and such. He and his wife once had a small store at the farm where we were working the press and while we took turns working, someone looked around in the old store. In one corner were what looked to be very old fireworks: Roman candles and large rockets. We wondered how safe they were but kept right on working with the apples. Later in the day, after the apples were done, raw cider was put away, and we had cleaned up, Steve came out with a large piece of pipe and one of the rockets and said, "We need to try one!" We all agreed.

The pipe was held at an angle, up toward a hill. The rocket was lit and dropped down the pipe. For a moment nothing happened, then suddenly it took off, shooting up onto the hillside where the milk cows were grazing. It landed right among the cows, exploded, and set the grass afire. The cows went in all directions. We headed up the hill as fast as we could, stomping out the flames as we went, as the rocket had left a trail of sparks. Coming back, we cleaned up our rocket mess and left. We thought everything was under control. Later that evening, Emil figured out what we had done when he found the burned patch and did not easily find his cows. Sunday morning I heard about it from my father and Monday, the class heard about it, much to our chagrin. Monday at lunch time, we all headed to Emil's gas station to apologize for our behavior.

A week of warm, very warm weather settled in the area. During study hall and other quiet times, we wondered how our cider was doing. Had we made it too early? What if we had to redo the whole batch? The cider was very important as it would primarily pay for the Junior-Senior Prom and

Banquet for which we were responsible. Saturday came and a few of us went out to check our cider. We found it covered with this moldy, bubbly stuff. It did not look good; in fact, it looked terrible! We thought we could skim most of the moldy, bubbly stuff off, which we did, and then we worried about how we were going to sell this stuff. We didn't even want to taste it. Collectively we decided we would skim what we could and on Wednesday a few of us would skip school, come out and press some more to add to the concoction. Our thinking was that if it had started to turn to hard cider, we would dilute it so no one would know. That meant getting permission to use the cider press again. Emil let us but we noticed the fireworks were gone.

The cider was a hit. It got rave reviews. People wanted to purchase jugs of it to take home. People kept coming back and purchasing more. We had many jugs but also some tubs as we ran out of jugs for all of our cider. Selling by the cup at the Jamboree would not stop. We kept refilling our pouring jugs from the tubs. We kept hearing, "This is the best cider ever." We just kept refilling and smiling. No way did we want anyone to know what we had done and how we prepared this great apple cider, maybe slightly hard. We kept the jug on our arm and lifted our elbow to fill the cups. We enjoyed our success but had to look ahead to the Prom and Banquet.

However, for my family the night did not end. The carnival had taken in a few thousand dollars and was in our house, under Mom and Dad's bed. Dad always felt the money was safer there than in the old school safe. Mom stayed awake most of the night waiting to be robbed. In the morning Dad was off to Baker to make the deposit since North Powder did not have a bank. Then came the job of cleaning up. The 1955 Cider Jug Jamboree had been a great success.

For my family, the Cider Jug Jamboree had started during the summer. Dad met with a company from Baker and selected the prizes for the games of chance. He ordered the gold fish in fish bowls, kewpie dolls of all sizes, trinkets for key chains, golden horses and stuffed animals of all sizes. The company gave Dad a calendar, or rather he thought it was a calendar, in a brown envelope, the size that would hold a company calendar. He brought it home and put it on the table.

Somewhat later I saw the envelope and pulled out the calendar. What a calendar! The calendar picture was a copy of the 1949 Marilyn Monroe nude calendar. I let out a yell, "Dad, way to go; can I hang this in my bedroom?" That got his attention and he put it away in his desk. It never saw the light of day unless the rest of the family was away from the house and I could check it out.

139

Prom

WE HAD MOVED TO NORTH POWDER that summer of 1951, where I started the seventh grade. Our class was small, only ten students. Our teacher, Mr. Irons, put us in alphabetical order, so there she sat, right in front of me.

Her name was April Spring.

I first noticed her when the school bell rang and we all walked into the classroom. She was very cute — though I mumbled to myself about her height — and I knew I wanted to get to know her. But this sitting right behind her was too fast. Our desks were in rows connected together by cast iron sides, with the top of the desk formed by the back of the seat ahead, which meant April was very close, not even space between our desks. When papers were sent down the row she didn't even turn around, just handed the papers back over her shoulder. I suspect she thought of me as nothing more than the new kid in class. I knew she would be a long-term project.

The April project was also going to be difficult. Our seating arrangement changed, though I was really pleased when she and I were in the same small group. I would have done my work and all of hers if she wanted. I offered to help her with some of her homework, but she never asked. She got good grades on her own. I admired her penmanship; she knew the Palmer method well.

140

I hoped to have a conversation with April at recess, but she always spent her free time with her girlfriends or the eighth-grade boys. I did get to dance with April once a week during Friday dance class. The rule was you could not refuse whoever asked to be your partner, so I made sure I got there first at least once.

When we entered eighth grade things changed. We were no longer in a self-contained classroom, but moved from one class to another with the high school students, thanks to a new schedule designed by the principal — my dad. It meant we lost recess time, but we did have time between classes. Most of our classes were together so I was able to keep track of April, though it meant the high school boys saw more of her, too. April did not appear to be as tall as I remembered from the previous year.

April lived on a farm and I thought maybe I could help her with her chores, but since I had few farm skills maybe it wasn't such a great idea. I did ride my bike out past her family's farm and was always ready to wave or even yell, but I never seemed to see her.

When I started high school the next fall, I became involved with football and math and sciences, while April was into home economics and sewing. We had social studies and English classes together, and what would become important to me... Study Hall. During Study Hall we began to talk of many things, though all too often the subject was an older boy. Often during Study Hall she visited with her girlfriends, giggling and having a good time, while I tried to ignore them and do my math. I realized that I was now just about as tall as April and on Friday I made sure we danced a slow dance.

By sophomore year we had become good friends. Life was changing for her. She said her brother was old enough to do most of her chores on the farm, so now she was cooking and sewing a great deal more. She laughed as she commented,

"You never seem to ride your bike out by my place anymore. You know, you could have helped me with my chores." I sat there, dumbfounded.

We only had a few classes together, but we still had Study Hall. We now spent most of the time talking about the guys she was dating. I was now a little taller than April, but she had begun developing in different places. All I seemed to develop was a bad case of acne.

By junior year, we were the best of friends. I was dating, but had to use the folks' car. The boys April went with had their own fixed-up rods. I would see her riding around with them. It wasn't fair. She had become a very beautiful young lady who everyone wanted to be with, though from my view, she had little skill in picking out the right ones to date. She always seemed to be attracted to the ones who hurt her, like a moth to flame. I kept wanting to say, Look at me, I will not hurt you, but I never did.

I did have close moments with April … in my mind. Late at night I would listen to "Shakey's Pizza Parlor Request Hour" on the radio coming from San Francisco and dreamed we were there together. When I later listened to "Lucky Lager Dance Time," she and I were dancing. Dance time always closed with "I'll See You in My Dreams." Even though I may have just gotten home late from a date, April was always in my dreams.

By our senior year April was dating an older boy in college. She could hardly wait to graduate so that she might attend the same college. She would major in fashion and they would have a whirlwind romance. I kept telling her he was not the one for her, but it was like blowing in the wind; she did not hear me. She looked forward to Christmas break — and later — spring break to spend all her time with him and then he would make a special trip home to take her to the 1957 Prom at Powder Valley High.

It did not happen. Everyone could have predicted it; he was such a jerk. I found this out in Study Hall, the first day back from spring break. She was devastated.

"April," I said, "would you go to prom with me?"

She looked at me as if she had never seen me before. "Yes, but why haven't you ever asked me before?"

I responded, "I never thought you would go with me!"

Before the day of prom we had dated two or three times, usually taking in a movie. I always went to the door to see if she was ready, which she always was. I always walked her to my folks' car, opened and closed the door for her, held her hand at the movie, stopped at the Little Pig Drive-in to have a coke, then take her home. I always walked her back to her front door and I think on the third date, got a little kiss. I was elated!

The night of prom arrived. I had washed and cleaned the car and was wearing a suit. I bought a corsage to match her dress. Her father opened the door and invited me in to wait. We were talking briefly when April came into the room, followed by her mother. April was beautiful! She made me pin on the corsage, but I was trembling so much, I didn't do it very well. April's mom beamed as she adjusted the corsage and off we went to an evening that I had been dreaming of for six long years. We were the surprise date of the prom. We were not the King or Queen, but I felt like the King for the night and knew she was my Queen.

The Ruler and the Ditch

JUST BEFORE DUSK in the summer of 1956, several friends and classmates of Powder Valley High School, boys and girls, had gathered at the football field to throw the football around and visit. The football field was just across the street from our house. As dusk fell and it became darker my mother came out of the house and called us together. She had just been called and told that our friend and classmate, Bill, had been hit by lightning. She told us he had been hit on the head while driving a tractor; the tractor was well grounded and the lightning bolt passed right through Bill. It looked like he would survive, though he would have to spend considerable time at the hospital. We gathered together in a tight group and talked about Bill. We were very concerned for him, but also his vital role in the football season ahead. He was the center of our six-man football team.

Almost a week later a few of us were allowed to see him at St. Elizabeth's Hospital in Baker. For the first few days the doctors did not allow him to even move as they wanted his neurological system to heal. When we were allowed to see him, he was past the most dangerous period. He wasn't allowed to move much, but we could visit. A great deal of our concern was expressed in a joking, nervous way.

Boyd asked, "Are you going to make it back for football?"

Steve said, "What a way to get out of work on the farm."

I asked him, "How is the old brain working?"

All our comments were just nervous chatter that meant very little. We had noticed many young nurses' aides coming and going and someone asked, "Do you always get this much attention?"

Bill very quietly motioned for us to come close. "The problem is I cannot move. These young nursing aides give me a sponge bath. That's all right until they start washing my privates. Then I start getting an erection. When the erection starts a nun, who oversees the action, pulls out a wood ruler and slaps it."

The three of us were aghast. "No, No, oh!" we responded. "How could they?" we said almost in unison. The news took care of much further discussion. We commiserated with Bill. "Just hang loose," or "Think of getting back to football." Then, as we were riding home we began to wonder about the ruler. Did the nun use the thick side? Did the nun use the thin side with the metal strip? Perhaps she used the flat side? Oh, the horrors of it all. We were all pretty sure if that part was working, other parts would soon heal. Then Steve said, "If he really got lucky, would it be an electrifying experience?" We roared!

Bill did make it back, played football, and even caught a scoring pass from his center position. In six-man football the center is always eligible. We had fun with the notion of the ruler; for most of the fall, someone could slap a ruler in his hand and all the guys chuckled. The girls in class always asked why were we laughing. No one ever shared the story.

Eastern Oregon in the fifties suffered under a plague of jackrabbits. Jacks were everywhere! The game department was giving bounties for coyotes. A pair of coyote ears could get you $5.00, which when wages were less than a dollar an hour, sounded pretty good. The results of having fewer coyotes meant a plague of jackrabbits. During Study Hall one day, five of us decided we should help the farmers by shooting as many jacks as we could. The ground was frozen, but we had no snow, a rare event. We decided to go spot lighting that night; it was a Friday night. Football was over and basketball games had not started so we were all free to go.

Lucky volunteered his car, a mid-1950s model, a Buick Roadmaster. He had a two-door hardtop type with, most importantly, two mounted spot lights with the controls on the inside and the light outside, one on each side of the car. He also had a handheld spotlight that plugged into the cigarette lighter socket. Seeing the jacks would not be a problem. I am sure none of us mentioned what we were doing to our parents. I left the house with my single shot 410 shotgun with a pocketful of ammunition. I know we had another 410 along and three 20-gauge shotguns. We were loaded for bear but hunting jacks. We met Lucky in front of the high school and were sorry to see he had brought his cousin along, a little older and bossy; he thought he knew it all and was a real jerk whom none of us thought of very highly. Before we even left the high school, Lucky's cousin indicated that the front of the hood was his seat, no discussion. That did not set too well with the rest of us, but we all piled into the car.

Lucky drove to a wheat field several miles out of town. We didn't want the town people to hear all the shooting we had planned. They might come and investigate. We established our positions. I would have the passenger side rear seat, Loren would have the driver side rear seat, Steve would have the driver side front fender, Billy would have the passenger side front fender and Lucky's cousin would sit on the hood, straddling the hood ornament. Lucky and Boyd would handle the spot lights. We drove through part of the field and all seemed to go well; lots of jacks, lots of shots, very few confirmed hits, but we were having a ball. Shooting from a moving vehicle while driving through a stubble field was much harder than we thought.

We stopped, discussed the situation, and decided to try one more line of attack. This time there were even more jacks going in all directions. Suddenly the Buick came to an abrupt stop! The front wheels were in a field wash ditch that ran through the stubble. The Buick stopped hard and fast. Loren and I pitched forward but were stopped by the seat in front of us. The spot lighters also went forward but stabilized themselves. Steve and Billy slid forward off the fender into the stubble. Lucky's cousin stayed right where he was. The crotch of his pants had hung up on the hood ornament. Immediately he was yelling and moaning. He was in a world of pain, still hung up on the ornament.

We were all laughing so hard it was a minute or two before we realized he was really hurting. We helped him down and he lay on the ground, all the time moaning and groaning. We encouraged him with words like, "Maybe they will have to amputate?" "No," someone said, "He will have to be castrated." "No, he will just walk strangely and speak with a real high voice." Lucky said something about getting him to a doctor, which sobered us all up, and we began to figure how we were going to get the front wheels out of the ditch. We kicked the dirt out behind the front wheel and with all of us pushing — well, all but one — and with rocking, we got the car out. We quickly piled in and headed for home. Lucky dropped us by the school and took off with his cousin.

We never saw the cousin again. Lucky said by the time they got home, he was through moaning and any hospital was forty-five minutes away, so they didn't do anything. His cousin and family left the next day. The cousin told Lucky he was black and blue and ready to go home. We had just started, however; no longer was it the slap of a ruler that created a break in the classroom routine. Now someone would groan aloud and a smile and chuckle came over all. Everyone at Powder knew what had happened. This helped get us through the long cold winter of North Powder. By spring we were much more mature and did not need these frivolous thoughts and ideas. We were graduating.

Sports at Powder

"LET'S GET MOVING!" Dad would say. He was our basketball coach, principal, and superintendent, but for right now, our coach. "We have lunch in Elgin at noon," he finished.

Billy asked, "Chicken fried steak and gravy?"

"Yes," Dad replied, "but we need to be there! Make sure you have your powder blue uniform in your bag. You might want to play!" He was pushing us to get on the bus as we were on our way to Joseph, a team we thought we could beat. The six seniors, our varsity, were wearing our new raglan sleeved, tweed top coat. We looked pretty darn sharp. The top coat covered our black with orange trim letterman sweaters and we each carried our own powder blue sports bag. We had to be in Joseph early enough for the JV game, which would take place before the varsity. Cheerleaders and most of the high school student body were making this trip. We'd get back home around 1:00 a.m. Win or lose, we had to stop in Elgin to get a hamburger on the way home.

The powder blue and white school colors were the result of a student body vote the previous spring. Four schools in our league had black and orange as school colors so we decided to change after seeing some great looking powder blue and white uniforms at the state basketball tournament. We wondered how the Powder student body had not chosen powder blue many years ago. We would still be the Badgers!

Powder Valley High was one of the smaller schools in 'B' classification in Northeastern Oregon. Our league included Joseph, Enterprise, Lostine, Wallowa, Elgin, Imbler, Cove, Union, St. Francis of Baker, Halfway, Richland, Hereford, and Huntington. North Powder was close to the center. Looking at a map, many of the teams we played had long trips by bus often over snowy roads and mountain passes.

In 1953 Powder Valley had 65 students and was playing 11-man football, basketball, and had a track team in the spring. We had 24 out for football and were able to be competitive with those in our league, winning half of our games. There were four freshmen on the team who did not contribute a great deal but allowed for some scrimmaging and holding blocking dummies. I will testify that those seniors loved to run over those freshmen holding those dummies. As a freshman Steve made the basketball varsity while the rest of the freshmen were on the JV squad. In the spring, very few turned out for track as most of my classmates had to go to work in the fields at home. I liked running distance and during the season did okay at the mile; at least I never got passed.

One memory of track still haunts me. At the district track meet, I was entered in the mile. Most of the runners had crossed the finish line and another young boy and I were dueling it out to see who would be next to last. The crowd had noticed us and everyone, it seemed like everyone, began to yell and encourage us. As we rounded the last corner I could feel and see that I was beaten. I felt pure terror looking toward the finish line and seeing all those people. Last, to finish last! I pulled up and ran into the infield. Immediately I realized it would have been better to finish last than to have quit. I had quit! I felt the air and noise leave the crowd and heard the round of applause for the boy finishing.

I saw Dad's face as he came up to me and asked if I was

okay. "You were way ahead of your best time ever," he said, looking at his stop watch. I knew I was never going to be really okay by quitting.

By 1956, my senior year, Powder Valley was down to fifty students and fifteen for football. We were playing six-man football. At least we could scrimmage. The rules were a little different with two ends, a center, two running backs, and a quarterback. Before the ball passed the line of scrimmage there had to be an open pass or lateral. The quarterback could not cross the line of scrimmage before lateraling or passing. Everyone was eligible to receive a pass, including the center. The defense had to count two seconds before crossing the line of scrimmage. It sure made for open field running and tackling. We had four downs to get fifteen yards in order to get another first down. Touchdowns were worth six points, run or pass for one point, a drop kick extra point was worth two and a drop kick field goal was worth four points. Needless to say, the game was wide open, scores tended to be high, and the school with the fastest running back seemed to win most games. Powder did not seem to have any breakaway speed. We won one game and lost the rest, usually scoring zero points, which was unheard of in six-man football.

I remember one touchdown-stopping tackle. The first game of the season, we were playing the Herford Bulls on their pasture-like field. They had a strong runner who broke through the line and was heading for a touchdown. He decided to run over me instead of heading around — his mistake. I made the tackle of my football career. The reaction of my teammates made it great.

Boyd was the first one over, yelling, "Way to go, Bob, way to go."

Billy and Craig slapped me on my shoulder pads. As we got set up for the next play Bill and Steve gave me the thumbs up. The whole team was fired up. It did not last long as we lost to Herford 48 to 0.

For the last game of the season we visited the Imbler Panthers with the winner going on to a district playoff. I am not sure how that was possible as the Mighty Badgers had only won the one game. At the start of the game it began to snow. They moved our bus up along the side lines for anyone not in the game to have a place to keep warm. Snow was coming down in those great big, wet flakes and it kept on coming down. By halftime we were playing in two inches of snow and it was still coming down. By the start of the fourth quarter we had four inches of snow and any semblance of the game was lost. Both teams were slipping and sliding with little control of what we wanted the do. The refs were guessing the sidelines, the line of scrimmage, or where one was tackled or started to slide. Everyone was soaking wet and cold. We lost 21 to 0 but the best thing was, our season was over! Now on to basketball!

We were primed for basketball as we thought we would be a contender for the league crown. The team had twisted Dad's arm to be our coach. I stayed out of the discussion but was very pleased. Last year's coach had moved on. I'm sure Dad didn't need more to do, but I know he was pleased, too. The team was elated. All six senior boys had played together since the seventh grade and we were close. We did not have a tall center but we were all around 6 feet and we were considered a tall team. Getting back into the gym, we were ready to make up for that lost football season.

Basketball was a major attraction in North Powder. Supporters came early to get their favorite seat. They came for the JV game, then waited while the varsity warmed up. A pep band was at every game and those in band and not playing basketball were expected to play in the pep band. The twins, Shanna and Sharon, were our cheerleaders. The new powder blue and white uniforms were a big hit with the students. The community mumbled and grumbled about the new uniforms colors but basketball was still the best entertainment around. The gym had three rows of riser seats on the floor level. It had a balcony with five rows of riser seats on the side and on one end. The noise could be deafening with the pep band playing, fans yelling, and cheerleaders from both schools trying to lead yells. The crowd went wild with excitement. To walk to the foul line, the place became still. What a thrill.

The season did not go quite the way we had planned. A missed shot here or there, a lost rebound, not having a tall center, all hurt. Steve's knee cost us a couple of games. He wore a knee brace but even so, the knee popped out of joint and each time it seemed to be in a critical situation. We would call time out, one teammate would grab his leg above the knee and another would grab his leg below the knee and pull. Popped back into place, he might sit out for a couple of minutes, then he would be back in the ball game. As the season drew toward the end we were playing pretty good ball. We thought we could salvage the season as we had to play in a sub district tournament and then play the winner of the other side's sub district tournament in a final game to see who would go on to state. So we had a chance.

Our first game was against Enterprise, the school where I had gone to the first grade. Was this some kind of karma? What did this mean? We had lost twice to Enterprise during the season but always felt we were the better team. The tournament was being held in Wallowa, which had a new gymnasium. I can remember sitting with Mom and Dad, watching the tournament, visiting with parents and students who had been classmates that first year of school and would soon be playing against each other.

The game was close all the way and the score went back and

forth with one team leading by a few points and then the other team leading. Steve's knee held up for the game and in the last few seconds, we were only down by two points. Steve intercepted a pass and I broke for our basket. He got the pass to me and as I drove to make the lay-in I was hammered by one of Enterprise's players. No foul was called and time ran out. We couldn't believe it; no foul? We were in shock! I should have had a two-shot foul opportunity, but we did not have a chance to tie the game. It was over.

That was the longest bus ride home. The "no call" was the talk of the school for many days. "No foul!" A week later Dad received a church news letter from a minister who had been at the game and was not rooting for either team. His newsletter congratulated us on our sportsmanship. He could not believe the refereeing of the game. It took away a little pain as we now knew, for sure, we had been robbed.

Spring time at Powder Valley usually meant no spring sports. Just one or two of had been interested in track. I had run during my sophomore and junior years but nothing outstanding. After doing some talking, we decided we could get enough out to play baseball. Now baseball weather we did not have, but you never knew for sure. The high school had the equipment because it used to have a team. There was a diamond with a backstop screen. We even had a graduate or two who would come back, not to play, but to help us out. Dad found us a coach from the teaching staff, so we began working and throwing the ball. Most of us had to purchase gloves and Dad got us a limited schedule. We thought we could have some fun with it.

After a couple of weeks of practice, on a Friday night with no school activities, my friends and I were just hanging out. Later in the evening someone suggested we go check out the parking places. The purpose was to see who was out and around and give them a bad time. About the second spot we looked, down by the depot, we found the baseball coach's car and one of our high school classmates. This whole thing got serious very quickly and we knew enough to leave. Getting home, I woke up the folks to talk to Dad. I told him we had found the coach making out with one of the students. Monday morning, we had a substitute teacher, no coach, and no baseball. He was fired and was gone from Powder. Our sports seasons came to an end. It did not turn out like we wanted but it was still good. Boyd and Billy had been named League All-Stars in basketball, there were some highlights and some downs we were still upset about, but we seniors were ready to move on.

"No Foul!"

Mary Lou and the Elk

"BOBBY, BOBBY, BOBBY, are you all right?" Mary Lou was screaming. "Oh! my God, what have I done?"

I was shaking my head, wondering why she was screaming. We were only six feet apart but she sounded so far away.

"I didn't mean to shoot you," I heard her say.

"I think you missed but you sure put a hole in the tailgate of your father's truck." I began to come back to normal, realizing her rifle had gone off, pointing in my direction. She had been fiddling with her lever action, hammer rifle as we were talking and it fired. "As an experienced gun user, how are you going to explain the hole in the pickup and almost hitting a friend?"

I had been walking up this old logging road on the first day of deer season when I came up to Mary Lou. She was sitting on a box, right behind the cab of her dad's pickup. Because a snack and a break were in order, I stopped to visit. I had climbed up and sat on the opposite edge of the pickup bed. After a brief review of the lack of hunting success and not hearing much in the way of shooting, school became the topic of discussion. We had gone to school together since the seventh grade and we were now seniors.

I thought this was a good time for me to leave. I wanted to be gone when her dad showed up and found a rifle hole in

156

the tailgate of his fairly new pickup. I did not want to get in the way of her explanation. I started back down this old road and thought I would cut through a thicket area, look over the land that opened below me, and have a chew of my Big Hunk candy bar. Sometimes it is your good fortune to be where you are, when you are. I was sitting on this stump when a young buck ran into the area, stopped, and had no idea that I was near. Twenty minutes after first seeing Mary Lou, I had survived a shooting incident and downed a buck that ran to ten feet of the road and dropped. Maybe I had better date Mary Lou, as long as she did not bring a rifle along on the date.

For a date I decided to take Mary Lou to La Grande to go bowling, which was an inexpensive date. The bowling alleys were in the basement of a downtown building, four lanes, with pin setters. We laughed a lot and had a good time as we bowled our three games. Of course, I tipped our pin setter. We left and went to the In-N-Out drive-in. We had something to eat, probably hamburger, fries, and cokes, then drove around Eastern Oregon College to look it over, though neither of us planned to attend EOC. We started home, kind of late, with just a few flakes of snow showing on the windshield.

In 1956, the main highway, which eventually became Interstate 84 between North Powder and La Grande, was a two-lane road over the top flat land and down through Ladd Canyon. Historically, this was the route of the Oregon Trail and Ladd Canyon was considered one of the most hazardous portions of the trail. Logs were attached to the covered wagons to slow their descent. Mary Lou and I were now getting a little concerned as we seemed to be in an early blizzard as we headed up Ladd Canyon. When we reached the top of the canyon, we were in a full-scale blizzard. No other traffic was on the highway. It was an eerie situation. As we continued across the top of the high plains we saw the lights of a large truck heading our way. As we got close to each other, we saw a herd of elk crossing in the head lights. We slowed to a stop, but not fast enough. We knew we were in extreme danger and both of us were yelling. All the elk moved except the one right in the center, which seemed frozen in the head lights of both oncoming vehicles. At the last second it stepped in front of the truck.

I stopped the car. The truck stopped. I backed up and got out to talk to the driver. He was looking over the front of his truck and could see no damage. We both walked back to the elk lying on the edge of the highway, dead. The truck driver had a large knife, cut its throat so the blood would drain, and told me I should throw it in trunk of the car. With Mary Lou in the car I did not think it was a smart thing to do. We pulled it a little farther over the edge, then we both took off. I needed to get Mary Lou home as I was going deer hunting early in the morning with Dad and a neighbor on the last weekend of deer season. On the way home we talked of how lucky we were the elk moved in front of the truck. We also joked some as Mary Lou was going out hunting with her father, but we were headed in opposite directions.

Very early the next morning as Dad, the neighbor, and I were leaving the house, I told them of the elk in the highway and how one had stepped in front of the truck and the driver had taken care of it. We quickly decided we should look over the situation, so we headed toward the high plains before Ladd Canyon. We found the carcass, protected and preserved by the snow and cold, right where I had left it and the scavengers had not found it. It was a spike and looked like the damage had been to the head. There was still no traffic on the highway so we loaded it into the trunk of the car. Moving quickly, we headed back toward North Powder, reached a back road and stopped close to the garbage dump, and gutted the elk. Putting it back into the trunk of the car we headed home and the old barn behind the house. We backed the car into the barn, removed the elk's head, hung it from a rafter, and skinned it. I took the hide and the head back to the dump. Now it just needed to hang for a few days.

The reality of the situation then took place. None of us had an elk tag nor was it even elk season. Dad was the district superintendent and high school principal and our neighbor was the elementary principal. This elk could become very expensive if news got out. I knew who would be taking the fall. Neither of my sisters were told what was in the barn as they could not be trusted not to talk at school with 'show and tell' time. The weather was cold so hanging in the barn was no problem. The elk aged and I am sure the folks aged right with it. A few days later the elk was cut and wrapped in the kitchen as we could not take this carcass to the butcher to cut and wrap. It was a big relief to get it into the locker and out of the barn and the house. We all breathed easier.

Over the next few months the elk was eaten and strangely, it never had the venison sagebrush taste we all were used to, as we often had venison but seldom elk. But the story never became part of the family lore of hunting. Afterwards, the event was never mentioned. I will tell you, it was so good and not a morsel was wasted. That one winter, we ate a little better.

Floating the North Powder River

IN LATE SPRING 1957, Boyd, who lived close to the North Powder River, came to class talking of the amount of water going under the bridge. He wondered if it was possible to float the river. That got Steve, Billy, and me discussing the possibility of making this float. We had all fished it many times and knew that in a couple of places barb wire fences crossed the North Powder but beyond that we could not think of a reason why we could not float the river. The North Powder flowed into the Powder River and at the confluence of the two we would need to make sure we could get out before we entered Rattlesnake Canyon. We had all been warned enough not to go to Rattlesnake Canyon.

The discussion of the trip went on for many days and more of our classmates were taking part in the discussion, some saying no way while others saying it should work. We knew that in October many years ago, an outhouse was lassoed by a couple of cowboys, tipped over with someone in the outhouse, and dragged by horse to the North Powder River and set afloat. If it could be done in an outhouse then surely it could be done in a rubber raft. I think Steve was the one who said he had this old, World War II rubber raft that we could use if we wanted to try it. This certainly upped the level of discussion.

160

Friday turned out to be a very warm day and we all thought if this was ever to be done, now was the time to do so. Boyd, Steve, Lucky, Billy, and I began this great adventure. We skipped Study Hall to get going a little earlier. I went home to get some seat floats. Steve headed home to pick up the raft and the pump. We had no real oars but had some slats from a picket fence that we thought would work quite well. Soon we were together at the bridge near Boyd's place and were pumping up this old high-sided ocean rescue rubber raft. It was going to be the Titanic of river rafting. We just didn't know how much we were going to be like the Titanic.

"Dang, it took a long time to pump up this raft," I said as I gave over my pumping to Boyd. It was hard work. We all noticed we could never seem to get the raft fabric very tight. We heard some air escaping and soon decided we would take the pump along and would pull ashore and add some more air if needed. We found we had one oar and a number of slats. Besides, we were just doing the North Powder River. What could go wrong? All we had to do was step ashore.

We soon were off; Steve, Billy, Lucky, Boyd and me, five guys in a tub. Within a few minutes we found the pickets were not of the highest quality; they splintered and broke as we turned around and around. Luckily or good thinking, we had spares. We had not gone far when we realized we were going to have a long walk back to our cars. Within a quarter of a mile we encountered our first fence across the river, but we knew that fence was not barb wire, but rather 4-inch wire squares. It shouldn't have been a problem but we had not yet managed to control the raft as the cold water and leaking air made it impossible to move around in this limp raft. When we hit the fence, we were right in the middle of the river. We soon learned the physics of moving water holding the raft in place. We could not believe how hard we raced to rescue the raft and how wet we were getting, especially since we were laughing so hard. Getting serious, we worked the raft to one side, lifted it across the fence, refilled with air the best we could and jumped back in, ready to go.

We continued to move down the river, seeing a fishing hole or two that we recognized from this new vantage point. We were able to cut down the spinning but we still had little control. We knew there were no rapids, just some faster moving riffles where we felt the rocks as we passed over them. The raft seemed to be losing air faster than we had thought it would. We tried to pump while we were moving along and found that did not work. We saw a barb wire fence ahead of us and managed to get to one side. We pulled the raft out, though now we had water in the raft and that was not so easy. Some of the frivolity of the trip had begun to disappear; not all, however. A little blaming came into the activity. We emptied out the water, got it across the fence, only snagging the raft once. After pumping it back up we were soon ready to go again.

We noticed now that the raft did not keep its shape at all and since we were close to the confluence of the Powder River, we knew we had to stay on the North Powder side. We knew that we were nearing Rattlesnake Canyon and none of us wanted anything to do with the canyon. With a great deal of effort, we worked our way into the Powder River, forcing ourselves to stay where were out of trouble. We neared an embankment that let us get to shore and up on the railroad tracks to walk home or to the highway to hitch hike.

Suddenly, whether the current picked up, somebody missed a grab on a bush, whatever, we were past our embankment, entering the jaws of Rattlesnake Canyon. Half of the raft was now flat, the other half was losing air, the pump had fallen overboard, the float cushions had floated away. We tried to push with the oar that had broken and most of the pickets were gone. We were enough in the jaws to see we were not going to rescue the Titanic. Time to abandon ship, try to stay along shore, keep a leery eye out for rattlers, and work our way back to the embankment we had spotted.

Steve said, "What am I going to tell my dad about his raft?" as we watched it move over rocks and into the channel and being swept down the river.

I said, "We can go to Andy and Bax," a famous army surplus store, "and buy him another. I am not going after that one!" Everyone agreed, even Steve.

After a half hour we were back to the embankment and climbing out. We had seen many sticks that we avoided, not knowing whether they were sticks or rattlers. We didn't see any in the water, and we knew they could swim. Nobody really wanted to be the first or the last in this line making our way back. But we had made it back. The mood lightened up once we knew we were safe, but it was late enough that we knew some parents might not be very happy. We decided to go to the highway and start walking. Maybe someone in a pickup would give us a ride … maybe.

Actually, Dad was the one who came to our rescue. He had heard rumors at school as to what we were doing and when we were late he decided to drive along the highway to see if he could find us. We were glad he did. Everybody got dropped off at their car or at home. No one's parents seemed overly concerned, figuring as seniors in high school we would eventually make the right decisions. We were pleased that Steve's dad was glad to get rid of the raft and we didn't have to replace it.

By Monday, almost all was forgotten. We all spent extra time working around the school to make up the Study Hall we had skipped. We were not heroes as most of our classmates wondered how we could be so dumb. Not because of the float, but we had let ourselves enter the Jaws of Rattlesnake Canyon.

Sexual Revolution: A Few Thoughts About Sex
at Powder Valley High

IN 1956, *Peyton Place* by Grace Metalious was published. By the fall of 1956, it entered the hallowed halls of learning at Powder Valley High. There were two book clubs at Powder that year; the other, *Lady Chatterley's Lover* by D.H. Lawrence. Neither book was part of assigned reading but were passed from student to student. The parts we really needed to study were dog-eared and well worn. Page numbers were memorized and passed along with the book.

The books were more interesting than biology class; maybe because of the atmosphere created in the books. Mrs. Osterloh, our biology teacher, tried to keep the idea of sex and the results of sex right out in front. She was pregnant every year and she always took the class through the whole process, except for a couple of days when the boys were not allowed in class and a couple of days later, when the girls were not allowed in class.

Because North Powder was an agricultural community, we all understood the role of the "birds and the bees." We had some ideas and basics about dating, which reflected the situation at Powder Valley High and living in North Powder. We learned to ask a girl out on a date at school, and not on the phone because our telephones were party lines and everyone would know exactly who and when we asked her out for a date. They knew immediately whether she said yes or no. The next day at school could be upsetting based upon what she said. Sayng yes was okay, unless someone thought we were cutting into his time. Party lines made it very sticky so it was better just talk to her at school.

Another basic was a young man always needed to be prepared. That meant he had to have two wallets. The first wallet was left out around the house, the one that contained money and class pictures, the one that Mom and Dad saw, the one we opened to show we needed to borrow some money. The one we left out for all to see.

The second wallet was never seen around the house but was seen at school or when we were hanging with the guys. The second wallet always contained a condom that was pressed into the wallet so its image showed on the outside along with a four-dot Olympia beer bottle label. Olympia beer bottles were all stubbies and the back of each label had from one to four dots. The hardest to find were the labels with four dots; they were very rare. We were under the belief that we could trade the four-dot label for sex. We never found any young ladies who subscribed to this theory but we needed to be prepared. It was probably a rumor started by Olympia beer to get the labels off of stubbies, making them easier to clean, and to sell more beer. Any time we saw an Olympia bottle with the label still on, we raced to get to that bottle and check the label.

The condom for the second wallet presented a little problem. North Powder had no drug store. One grocery store had some personal items, including condoms, that were kept behind the counter. The owner and only clerk had a daughter a year behind in school, very attractive and popular. The whole concept of purchasing condoms from him was not good. That meant trying to buy in Baker or La Grande, working a trade or finding a restaurant or service station restroom that sold from a dispenser. Trading an Olympia 4-dotter and some money might get a condom. But the one trading his spare condoms probably had lots of 4-dotters and little use for either of them; that old supply and demand thing.

The impression of the condom was kind of like a round snooce can carried in the back pocket of Levi's that left an imprint in the jeans. Keeping the condom this way created some wear on the condom package, tended to open the package, resulting in needing to find an immediate use for the condom. The most common; it became a water balloon that might be heaved at a passing car or might be hung over the antenna of a friend's car. Hanging it over the antenna needed to be done unobserved; being seen would create a problem. The bigger problem was now needing a new condom.

As TVs became more prevalent, we watched girls screaming over Elvis and other rock stars, and we could watch *American Bandstand*. We did not understand all that we saw but we noted the effect. With our "sox hops" after school on Fridays, more and more 'rock and roll' was being played on the 45s brought from home. We all enjoyed the time, but where did we belong? In senior pictures, most of the boys had flat tops, while the two who moved to North Powder later in their school career had DAs. The girls wore little sweaters with Peter Pan collars. Formal dances were still with dance bands playing the old standards.

James Dean helped create a rebellious attitude of how we were to dress, talk, and even act. He was someone unlike any of us knew. We were devastated when he was killed in a car accident in 1955. I remember talking with my classmates and believing the tabloid rumor of his being badly injured and taken to Mexico to be restored to health. I had a hard time giving up on his return.

By our senior year, very few had their own car. Double dating was an acceptable arrangement for my friends and me. There was little relationship between what went on in the front seat and what went on in the back. They were two separate worlds. The only real problem was who went home first; usually the date in the back seat, even if extra miles had to be traveled to make that happen. Once the backseat date was dropped off, the boy moved to the front seat and the other couple moved to the back seat. Whoever was in the front seat controlled the radio and in winter, the temperature. The temperature was the hard one as it tended to get very steamy inside the car. Afterwards, when both girls were home, we headed to downtown Powder. If both girls were Baker girls, we headed out to a truck stop café, ordered a greasy hamburger, put money in the juke box, and listened to Patsy Kline and Marty Robbins. A good time to remember.

Basketball season in Eastern Oregon had its own challenges, as we often had long bus rides. Almost all fifty students in Powder Valley High went to away games. Most of our opponents were 50 to 100 miles away. That meant long bus rides homes, in the dark, especially in the back of the bus. On the way, the girls had the back of the bus and the boys stayed in the front half. On the way home was a different story. To be sure, you needed to be a senior to sit all way in the back of the bus. Everything got mixed up as the senior boys tended to go with junior or sophomore girls. Senior girls, who always went to the games and last year sat in the far back now had to move forward and usually sat with other senior girls. The freshmen and sophomores got the front of the bus. Every once in a while, we heard a slap or a "stop that." The riders in the back of the bus roared with laughter while the front of the bus yelled and asked what was going on. Sometimes the bus driver turned on the lights and everyone straightened up, but as soon as the lights went out the process started again.

When the bus returned to Powder, the senior girls were off the bus in a flash. They were being picked up by older boys who had already graduated. The junior and sophomore girls waited for the senior boys to take them home. Being late, the girls often had to go right home. The boys who were taking girls home hoped a few minutes of 'parking' might be in their future.

'Parking' had its risks. There were not a lot of good places to park, especially in the winter, as we had to worry about road conditions, be it snow or mud. Nobody wanted to park where getting stuck might put a mark on our reputation. We all knew where the good spots were so if we were not so lucky because our girl had to go right home and our friend also did not have a 'parking' mate, we had a duty to drive around to see who was parked. We were easily entertained but what did we expect living in North Powder when gas was 25 cents per gallon.

Radium Hot Springs

IN LATE SUMMER 1864, Margret Lieuallen, my great great grandmother, asked her husband, William, the wagon master, "What was that odd smell and I don't mean the oxen that I have walked beside nearly two thousand miles?"

William, in an exasperated way responded with, "It's a hot water spring about a mile away toward the mountains that smells like rotten eggs."

Margret, "That is where we are camping tonight!"

William answered, "That means two miles out of our way."

Margret, "After all this distance I have walked from Missouri, you think I would mind another two miles?"

As the train made a turn toward the mountains, William thought, *Well maybe the women might enjoy the water in the hot springs. It has been very dusty since we came down the hill near Baker City. Maybe it will be a good place to rest overnight.*

In late summer, 1951, Dad loaded the family into the car to go to the Radium Hot Springs Pool. This was the first time the family went to a pool following my brother Donny's drowning. I know Mom was very worried and both Mom and Dad would be watching my sister and me like a hawk. Going into the pool we were given strict areas as to where we could play. I could go to the rope that divided the shallow end from the deep end but I could not climb on the faded

169

red tank of an old hot water heater. The tank, free floating, was attached to the sides of the pool by a thick rope. I could use the slide into the shallower water. Sister Lynne could go as far as the slide and the youngest, Dana, just two-years-old, stayed with Mom, playing in the kiddie pool. We had a great time and before we got out of the water Lynne and I asked for swimming lessons. The pool became the place where we spent a great deal of time, even when relatives visited.

On the way home from one of these trips Mom said, "I think your great great grandparents visited this area when they moved west."

The Radium Hot Springs Pool had been constructed near geothermal springs and in its early years was a spa with a hotel, which burnt, leaving only the pool. The springs were hot enough to boil eggs and the water had to be cooled from cold well water before entering the pool. Throughout Eastern Oregon there are several hot geothermal springs but the uniqueness of Radium was its location, right next to U.S Highway 30, the main east-west through-fare across Oregon. Many tourists loved to stop and camp for a night before continuing on their journey. The kids of North Powder viewed it as 'The Pool,' the only pool. My friends and I were at the pool a couple of times a week; a great place to visit and play when work was completed, usually after haying all day.

In late summer, 1956, Billy sat on that same faded red tank. Loren and Craig held the rope on one end of the tank while Bill and I were at the other end. With one arm raised as if he were going to ride a bull, Bill shouted "Go," loud enough that the girls at the other end of the pool looked up. The four of us began thrashing the rope as best we could, trying to buck Billy off the tank. His moment of fame did not last long as he soon found himself in the deep end of the pool. Being my turn, I had the same results, lasting no longer. By now the girls had moved closer and were asking about our ability to ride. We offered them a chance, told them we would take it easy, but they refused. Steve was next; he gripped the tank with his legs, someone gave it a spin, and he ended up with his head in the water and his feet on top. He didn't even get to say "Go."

We soon learned we were visiting with Baker girls. We did not get to visit with Baker girls very often as Baker had a large municipal pool. Once in a while Baker high schoolers, usually a party like a birthday party, ventured out in the evening to visit Radium. What a distinct change of pace when a group of Baker girls came to the pool. We had to be much more genteel; we might try to date one of them.

It wasn't long, however, before we were playing catch with some balls in the pool. Some dived from the low board, some jumped from the high platform doing a running cannon ball. Others were at the top of the slide ready to come down. The slider always tried to catch others unaware so the splash would get others soaked. Others were at the bottom of the slide helping out and encouraging. The testosterone level in the pool rose to new heights as a great deal of flirting and interaction took place. We talked like both sides were sampling forbidden fruit before going out the drive to the highway, turning in opposite directions, and never really expecting to see each other again. Maybe it was our version of teenage romance and checking out the girls. We thought it was right up there with the beaches of California, though we did no singing.

If the girls were Powder girls the action was much different. The Powder girls from our class tended to be more like sisters, as most of us had been together since the seventh grade. With the Powder girls, we were more physical like dunking and tackling from under the water. We knew we were going to get it back. Most were farm girls, used to working, and strong enough to take no sass. The twins,

Shanna and Sharon, would not stop until they had dunked us, especially when they were getting even. Sharon never stopped until we got out of the pool. Marilyn screamed as she attacked. Mary Lou waited to get even until we least expected it. Sometime during the evening the girls were on the guys shoulders ready to pull down the other pairs of combatants. We all had great times!

The evenings that were not great fun was when there were three groups: The Baker girls, the Powder girls, and the Powder boys. Not a happy scene. We avoided getting between the two groups of young ladies as daggers flew across the top of the water. Even though the Powder boys did not normally date our classmates, the girls in our class were very protective and I suspect a little jealous. When the girls were together at the pool, Powder girls did not like the guys talking to the Baker girls.

Once in a while there was some serious tension in the parking lot of the pool. Occasionally Baker boys followed Baker girls to Radium and took offense if we were spending too much time with the girls. We would say something about them trying to move in on the Powder girls but never anything very serious. Fighting words were usually spoken from the safety of the car as we were leaving the pool. The two schools did not compete in sports, as Baker was much larger, so these abrasive times were done and forgotten.

Sometimes, there were girls or boys from the campground who were just staying overnight. There the talk was mostly about traveling, where they were from and where were they going. They always knew we were local as we all had farmer's tans. It inspired and enlightened us as most of us did little or no traveling. Ones who stopped were often moving from someplace on the East coast to the Willamette Valley. None were ever moving to North Powder.

We always ended our evening with a bag of hot buttered

popcorn and we always suggested that the visitors stop by the treat window and ask for a bag of popcorn with butter and salt, the best treat ever invented. Enough butter would be poured over the popcorn that it would soak through the bag.

Oh, so good!

My Secret Place

I WAS SITTING ON A LOG at 'My Secret Place,' a secret place where I was at peace. The place where I could hear the wind from the wings of a butterfly and a short time later hear the wind passing through the Ponderosa pines. I could hear Little Antone Creek gurgling as it went down the canyon over the rocks and under the logs. Little birds flittered along the stream searching for insects. If I listened intently into the sound I swear I could hear the packers and mules traveling down the trail while the Downy Woodpecker worked on an old snag. I heard the mules, their hoofs creating a plucking sound as they crossed a corduroy part of swampy trail.

It became my secret place where I could sort out my thoughts. Where I would go to college? Was the Hungarian Revolution going to become 'my' war? How could black students be denied entry to a high school in Kentucky? What did I think of Elvis, Bill Haley, or Chuck Berry? Who would I take to the Winter Formal? These were some of the thoughts I tried to sort out in my mind as I sat on the log, listening and watching.

In the fall of 1952 when I was an eighth grader, this spot became my secret place when my best friend's dad, Bill, had suggested we try our luck on Little Antone Creek. He had fished it when he was younger where it reached the valley floor and crossed through his father's land. He hadn't fished it for many years and doubted if anyone else had. He indicated it required a hazardous trip down into the canyon and coming back up was equally as hard. He said the fish wouldn't be big, about the 10-to 12-inch size, wild and full of fight, especially using light gear. It sounded great!

A few days later Dad and I prepared to give the fishing a try. Preparations had to be made as we knew we wanted to take limited gear. Worms — we needed worms — so the day before Dad gave the lawn and a portion of the garden a good soaking. The garden gave up a few angle worms by digging and turning the soil. The lawn was much more lucrative as we had our old extension cord, end cut off, wires stripped and each wire wrapped around a large nail. With the nails poked into the wet lawn, the cord plugged into an outlet, we began collecting night crawlers. For some reason, they did not like the electricity flowing through them and would work themselves up to the top of the grass. They went into a bait can that was attached to our belt. We also wanted to take grasshoppers. The only way to get grasshoppers is early or late in the day. See one, bop it with your baseball cap, quickly grab and stuff into a Sir Walter Raleigh pipe tobacco can or a Prince Albert tobacco can. Grasshoppers chased with a little heat in the day were very seldom caught. A few extra hooks and shot weight and we were ready to go. We took split bamboo fly poles, but no flies, as we expected Little Antone to be very brushy.

Dad and I left North Powder and headed toward Anthony Lakes, turning off on a road that went beside Little Antone Creek. Soon the road began a sharp climb, with many switchbacks leading up through the Ponderosa pines. The area had been logged many years ago but many of the trees left behind were now very large. There was still some logging going on farther up the mountain so we were constantly alert for logging trucks coming down the mountain. The logging trucks, filled with three or four logs, moved quickly and took most of the road. More than once we had to squeeze by or back up to find enough clearance to get by. Eventually finding a wide spot, we parked, gathered our gear, and went over the side, a very steep incline; as we went over, we were thinking this might really be a bear coming back up.

When we neared the bottom of the canyon, the sound of the stream indicated we were right on track. The bottom of the canyon was about thirty yards across with the stream taking about one third of the space. Coming down the road side of the canyon we crossed an old pack trail used by the gold miners that ran from the gold fields north of Anthony Lakes toward Baker. These gold fields became known as China Diggings. There are many China Diggings in Eastern Oregon, so named because the white miners had creamed the gold from the fields. The areas were left for the Chinese to work and search for any remaining gold. Places along Little Antone Creek, down in the canyon, were quite marshy and I expect the Chinese cut small trees and laid the logs side by side, creating the corduroy trail, a common approach for trails and roads at the time.

We quickly started to fish. I heard Dad say, "I got one!" and I responded with, "So do I!" In thirty minutes, we both had our limit of rainbows — ten each. We had hardly moved from that first hole where we'd started. We were not quite ready to return to the car so we started looking around.

Standing at the sandy edge of the stream I looked down and saw the flicker of gold in the sand. I got down on my knees and peered into the water. I saw a few gold flecks, then I moved the sand with my finger and saw even more gold flecks. I yelled for Dad, "I think I found gold!" He came over to see my find and laughed, then let me know it was mica, 'fool's gold.' I was crushed as I had already begun to think we would be rich. That took some wind out of my sail.

Soon we were back up the hill to the car and then home. It was a great fishing trip, though it sure did not last long. The family certainly appreciated the fish feast that night for dinner.

We went back quite often, parking at the same place and over the hill, coming down close to the same spot. We fished up and down the stream, always catching our limit. Seeing the trail always got me thinking of the people who traveled the trail. I tried to picture them, standing as I was standing, and I questioned, *Where had they come from? Were they looking for gold? Why here, right here in this canyon? Did they find what they were after?* I know I soon learned to appreciate the solitude of the silence of the surroundings. And just downstream, I found 'My Secret Place.'

Dad and I made many trips to the Little Antone that fall and the following years. It was our place. We never really talked to others about the fishing and we never saw another person down in the canyon. I remember Dad, not lying, but maybe distorting where we went. The temperature was always at least ten degrees cooler and on the really hot days of summer it provided great relief; all we needed were bait and a couple of hours. In my later years of high school, I would go up alone and spend most of the day at my one spot, listening for the mules coming down the trail and the mule skinners calling out to one another.

Powder Valley High-Treasure Hunt

WE WERE NEAR THE END OF OUR SENIOR YEAR at Powder Valley High, 1957. We would soon be graduated and scattering to the four winds. Though we knew our time together was drawing to a close, we were all eager to go. I had asked Mom and Dad if I might have a party at the house and they were quick to agree, since most of my class had been together since the seventh grade. But with only fourteen in the class, I asked if could I invite a few others. Dad was adamant that we have no more than twenty. He would write a Treasure Hunt for four groups. I asked Mom to make sure April was in my group.

The date was picked and people were solicited to help. We soon had our twenty with six others selected who we felt were almost in our class. Mom took care of the refreshments while Dad disappeared back to school to write the clues uninterrupted. He had looked around Powder and developed spots where clues might be hidden. He then wrote a four-line verse that described, hidden in the verse, where the clue would be found. Each group would have to decipher the verse to know where to look for our next clue.

The night arrived for the party. It had been heavily discussed during the day and the entire class was attending. The girls were dressed in pedal pushers, tennis shoes with anklets, blouses with sweaters or jackets. The guys wore jeans, a button shirt and a White Stag jacket. We needed to be ready to quickly cover a lot of territory and our old Converse All-Stars were appropriate. Besides, who knew where we might step in Powder as only a few streets were paved.

Finally, the four groups of five were ready to rumble. We were off to the races! We were all on foot and we had to keep our group together. That first clue took all four groups to the arched entrance of the post office, which was in the center of town. It was a stone building with lots of nooks and crannies, especially good for hiding clues. Local lore claimed a drunken cowboy had butchered a young animal and hung it from the top inside the arch there and where Steve and I had picked up the newspapers for delivery when we were younger. There were clues for each group and we needed to find the right clue for our group. It was stressed and expected that we would leave the other clues alone. From the post office, each group headed in different directions but would, many times, cross paths.

One of the clues took us to the cemetery where shrieks, moans, and yells filled the dark night as juniors and seniors ran from one side of the cemetery to the other. Probably not a great deal of reverence was shown that night as we jumped out at each other having a great time. The groups' clue led to one that had been "killed in a gun fight." It was next to the large flat stone that one would rap and yell loudly, "What are you doing down there?" and it always answered, "Nothing."

One of the clues took us near the water tower. North Powder, like almost every town, had a water tower which was tall enough to provide gravity fed water to the town. Somewhere along the base we had to find our next clue. The water tower clue was also next to the city hall, the jail, and the fire station and that meant 'Speed,' the city sheriff who rode around in an old military jeep, would be close by watching for any shenanigans. With stealth, cunning, and avoiding Speed, we found our clues near the ladder that led up the tower. No way were we to climb the ladder this time.

One of the clues was down by the railroad track and depot. This was a really dark part of town. There were very few street lights in North Powder and the depot area was even darker. Like many old depots in the country, it had a loading dock on the side away from the tracks and a ticket window area. The Streamliner, with its passengers heading to all parts of the world, passed through but it didn't slow down, not even for one of our senior class members, as we all dreamed of something beyond North Powder. But with our flashlights now starting to give up the ghost, all the groups found their next clue.

One of the clues was by the flag pole of Powder Valley High, the same flag pole the class was going to put the upside-down garbage can on top of, emblazoned with 'Class of 57' just before we left on Senior Sneak Day. The flag pole was near an old outhouse's future location, the high school steps. This clue was harder to find as it took some looking, but the clue was right near the slide fire escape from the second story of the school. We all knew we were never to use this slide except in an emergency but who could pass on a steep two-story slide sliding on waxed paper.

One of the latter clues was near the church where Baccalaureate was to be held. We knew the service was an important step in the graduation process. A couple of North Powder ministers spoke, just to make sure we were on the moral side of our future. Of course, we all listened diligently and remembered the advice we would hear. In the shadows of the church, near the steeple end, each group found its next clue. That clue led to the entrance to the gymnasium in which we hoped to be seen in a graduation procession soon. We searched and searched with no avail. After closer rereading and studying the clue, we realized we needed to be near the door we had used so many times to sneak into the gymnasium. Whether we were playing basketball, volleyball, or just hanging around, the gymnasium was our center of activity. That door was just across the street from our home and looking back, Dad always knew where we were.

The last clue led to our home where the treasure was found. A treasure chest of gold-wrapped chocolate coins, but most importantly, caps and gowns for all the seniors. Most of our parents were waiting when we got back to the house. They had contributed some food and offered congratulations to all. After the parents left, we all went back to the gymnasium for our last sock hop and what a hop. Elvis led the way with "Jailhouse Rock," "All Shook Up," "Don't Be Cruel," "Heartbreak Hotel," and "Love Me Tender." Pat Boone was next with his "Love Letters in the Sand." The Everly Brothers sang, "Bye-Bye Love" and "Wake Up Little Susie," and Marty Robbins finished with "A White Sport Coat," and Ricky Nelson, "A Teenager's Romance," and many others, all of them on new 45s that our parents had recently purchased. Hands down, the best sock hop ever!

Graduation 1957

LATE MAY 1957 was graduation time for Powder Valley High School. Mr. Childers, the band instructor, had the band play the Processional as fifteen graduating seniors marched down the center of the gymnasium, up the stairs to the stage where we were sat, beaming. Marvin Vancil, Superintendent, (Dad) said a few words as he presented the graduating class of 1957 to the world. As Salutatorian, I had a few words that described some of the accomplishments of the class. Bill, the Valedictorian, warned the world that we were on our way. The Chancellor of Higher Education of Oregon, my uncle, gave a speech to the seniors as to our role in the world and how we had prepared for this time. The Chairman of the School Board presented us, one by one, our diplomas. As the Recessional was played we graduating seniors moved to the front of the gym floor. The town people of North Powder and the surrounding area came by to congratulate us all. Our graduation was a big deal for the community as they had followed us and our activities for many years. We broke into smaller groups but looked at one another, maybe moved to hug, then came back to our family. It did not really register that this would be the last time we were all together.

Our senior year had been so much fun, actually all four years had been good, but senior year was special. We had made it through football, six-man type. We had done okay in basketball but lost a heart breaker to Enterprise in the regional tournament that we believe kept us out of the state tournament. Boyd and Billy had been named to the all-star team, which was great. The senior Christmas dance had been a big success with the theme 'South of the Border,' a crepe paper ceiling improved the intimacy of the gym, a large barrel cactus around which we all danced. We had provided the leadership of the *Broadcaster*, the school newspaper, and the *Badger*, the annual. We had changed the school colors from orange and black to powder blue and white. We enjoyed the prom and banquet the junior class had created for us. We made it through the Cider Jug Jamboree, the school carnival. We had a couple of plays in which many of us participated and had leading roles. The band and chorus did well at State. Bill and I went to Boys State in Corvallis, Oregon. Most of us had college visits as we searched for the next step. We put a large garbage can, upside down, on top of the flag pole emblazed with "Class of 57." We also left an old dilapidated outhouse on the front steps of the school as we left on Senior Skip Day, heading for a day of fun and frolic in Walla Walla, Washington. And now we were graduating.

The emotions and feelings of being a senior were so strong, especially this year of 1957. Sitting in a brand new 1957 two-door hardtop Chevy Belair on the show room floor, we wondered how long before we could get something like this. Or at the Ford dealer, sitting in an Edsel, we wondered how the gear shift in the steering wheel was going to work as we all drove stick shifts. Maybe making a game-saving tackle or playing football in the snow at Imbler. Or lining up to start the basketball game with the cheer leaders yelling and the crowd alongside the gym floor and in the balcony screaming and clapping their hands. And then the thrill of winning a close game or the agony of losing one. After the game and a dance, going to Baker to have pork noodles at the Royal Café or going out to the truck stop, south of Baker, and having a great greasy hamburger and fries while listening to Marty Robbins singing, "A White Sport Coat and a Pink Carnation," and Patsy Cline singing, "Just Walking in the Rain," from the juke box and then just before leaving hearing Frank croon, "In the Wee Small Hours of the Morning." The hay rides, with most of the class aboard, whether at Marilyn's or right around Powder. Then there were the discussions about registering for the draft and knowing we were going to be One A and probably sent to Europe, unless we went to college and got a college deferment. All these decisions were being made by and for us and we could not even vote.

Or there was just hanging out at the Radium Hot Springs pool. Sometimes we pooled our quarters to buy a dollars' worth of gas that got us to Baker to watch a movie at the drive-in with some hiding in the trunk so we could get in cheaper and when we left would head to the Little Pig Drive-in for fries and a coke. Maybe coming back to Powder, parking along the street down by the Post Office and just talking. In late Spring, a cigarette might show up or even a six-pack of stubbies might be brought out if we could find someone to buy it for us.

Change was happening to us throughout our senior year. The kids from the Muddy Creek area joined us as freshmen. I remember Linda moving away but Boyd and Lucky joined us, while Tammy rejoined us. We were a very stable group, like a big family of brothers and sisters. We were together for most of our classes except for a few specialty classes like Home Ec., Shop and Advanced Math and Science. As we started looking elsewhere we began separating from each other as we were all heading to different futures. There were fifteen trails heading away from Powder Valley High and each would be obscured from the others and in all likelihood we would not pass this way again.

The outside world was changing for North Powder as well. More store fronts were becoming vacant. We lost a grocery store. We lost our telephone office. Television was entering the homes and would change our lives. The Cold War was very ugly and hatred ran deep toward the Soviet Union. A couple of the gypo-mills were closing and families that had worked in Powder were now moving to Baker or La Grande or the dad was commuting. Mothers were going to work, especially young mothers, as two incomes were needed. Yes, changing times began to erode the closeness of the fifteen who graduated in the spring of 1957 from North Powder and Powder Valley High, but what a journey we had getting to this special time.

Thanks: Billy, Steve, Lucky, Bill, Boyd, Loren, Marilyn, Shanna, Sharon, Gerry Rose, Tammy, Mary Lou, Edith, Lynn, and my special friend, April. Thanks for the memories!

After Graduation

Little Richard

MY CLASSMATES were spreading to the four winds. I suspected, with a twinge of the heart, that April and I were saying our last goodbyes. She was off with her parents on a long trip before going to school in the fall. Most of my classmates would be working at their dads' ranches until time for college. Boyd was heading into the military. Loren had hired onto a logging company. Gerri Rose was heading for Portland looking for a start in her career. The twins, Shanna and Sharon, were heading to Pendleton to work in the pea cannery. I was off to Weston to live with my grandparents and work the pea harvest.

Living with my grandparents was good as I knew I would be spoiled. Grandma always had my lunch ready, no matter what time I left in the morning, as well as having fixed me a breakfast of bacon, two eggs over easy, hash browns with two pieces of toast and homemade jam. She always said a working young man needed a great start of the day.

Besides working pea harvest, Weston had another attraction for me. Her name, Sharon! Sharon was an off-and-on girlfriend. On when I was in Weston and off when I was in North Powder. Hopefully, she saw me in the same way. Many hand-written letters passed back and forth through the mail, though we both were very much involved in our own high school life. It was nice and convenient and certainly nothing serious. She lived about five blocks from my grandparents so it was easy to spend time together while sitting on her porch. Neither of us had daily access to a car. Some days we walked to The Fountain, a soda and ice cream parlor. Occasionally I could use my grandfather's four-door 1939 Plymouth or when the folks visited I could use their car and Sharon and I might take in a movie in Walla Walla, Washington, or Pendleton, Oregon. But with both of us going to work early, being out really late was not usually an option.

Reading the newspaper was always important to me. At my grandmother's it was the *Walla Walla Bulletin*. Once while reading the paper I noticed an ad that Little Richard would be performing at the Walla Walla Armory on Monday, June 17. The same Little Richard who brought us such number one classic hits such as "Tutti Fruiti," "Long Tall Sally," and "Lucille." Talking it over with Sharon, we thought it would be a lot of fun to go. It soon became a quest to make it happen, but the dance and show would last until 1:00 a.m. and we both knew that was not going to work.

We could use Sharon's parents' car if Sharon's older brother would drive, which was also not going to happen. My granddad's response was, "Are you kidding me? You have to go to work Tuesday morning and I expect you to give a full day's work." The prospect of going looked bleak until Mom called on Sunday evening, a week ahead, and told Grandma she was coming over for a visit and to shop. That gave me my in. "Mom, could you stay one more night? It is very important! You would have more time to shop and visit with your sisters." Since Dad was not coming over it made sense to Mom so she quickly agreed. Transportation was a done deal; I could use the folks' car.

After telling Sharon the good news, we thought it would be more fun if we had a small group. We had double-dated a number of times with my cousin who lived in Umapine, Oregon, which was on the old highway to Walla Walla. Cousin Richard was all for it; he would have a date and we would be on our way.

Monday, June 17th came quickly. A decision had been made to have hamburgers at the Triple X Root Beer Drive-in in Walla Walla, before the dance. The Triple X featured window service, great hamburgers and fries, and frosty root beer mugs with head dripping over the side of the mug. How could life be any better than this? When we picked up Richard and his date and another shirttail cousin and her date, the six of us were on the way to a great time. The folks' Oldsmobile 98 could handle this gang.

We always knew when we were approaching the Triple X Drive-in. The building was built as three large kegs of root beer that were large enough to be part of the skyline coming into Walla Walla. That night the drive-in was a happening place and we soon joined the crowd. Maybe our plans were not so unique but we found a place to park, placed our order, and waited for the food. Our hamburgers, fries, and root beers were just as we had anticipated. It was approaching 8:30 as we finished so we needed to find a place to park near the armory and get inside for the start of the show.

When we arrived near the armory and started looking for a parking space we realized that maybe we should have arrived a half hour earlier. We had never anticipated anything like the crowd of people standing around outside and who knew what was inside. We were not deterred, however; we finally found a parking place and were soon standing in line to purchase our tickets. By now it was 9:00, the dance was beginning, and we were still waiting in line. We could hear the music but we were not in the door. Were we missing Little Richard, or was it really him? It just did not sound right. Finally, it was my turn to pay. I put down a $5.00 bill for Sharon and me. Such a deal with tickets being $2.00 each. I got my change and with tickets in hand we headed inside.

The armory was jam packed with more coming in. There must not have been fire marshal rules about the number people in the building. We could see a band on the stage but it didn't sound like or look like Little Richard. Slowly moving toward the stage, we found out that this was a warm-up band and our man would be later. The armory got very hot as we were dancing but not moving. Sweat was dripping from all with no breeze to cool us off. We decided to step outside. We even danced some outside, as it was not hard to hear the warm-up band. We decided that if Little Richard was going to make an appearance it would have to be soon. The six of us went back inside and created a little standing place fairly close to the stage and waited.

Suddenly the lights went out for a short time, a spot light came on, shining on the stage. A grand piano had been rolled to the center. The announcer yelled, "and here is Little Richard," stringing it out for a few seconds. He walked out of the darkness into the spot light glow in a green suit. We looked at each other, and then started yelling and clapping like everyone else. He broke out with "Rip It Up" and followed with "Girl Can't Help It" and now the crowd was fully alive and into the event. He said something, but we could not hear what he said. We looked at each other and shrugged our shoulders. He sang, "Long Tall Sally" and the crowd was even more energetic; the air was electric. When he sang "Lucille" we looked at each other and said this was all right. Then with the first syllables of "Tutti Fruiti," you could hardly hear him as the crowd went bonkers. Such a scene with everyone going wild, cheering, and yelling. Then he walked off the stage. He was through! We couldn't believe it; we had waited all this time to hear five songs. Five songs!

We could not understand when a different band came on to play. As we headed out we heard the announcer say something about Little Richard would be back later but we knew we had to leave.

The trip back to Umapine and Weston was very anticlimactic and we were all very quiet. We'd had a great time, but it just didn't end like we had expected. Even though we thought we had gotten our money's worth, there was a funny feeling that Little Richard had short-changed us. But we didn't have time to mourn too long as all six of us had to be at work early—very early that morning.

Goodbye April, Hello Sharon

GROWING UP IN EASTERN OREGON in the 1940s and 1950s, the name Til Taylor meant a great deal. Travelers driving through Pendleton, Oregon, on U.S. Highway 30, always pass a large statue of a sheriff on horseback. The question is always, "Who is this man?" From my parents, I heard again the story of Til Taylor. He had been a beloved sheriff of Umatilla County for many years who was gunned down during a jail break in 1920. More than a hundred-man posse, most on horseback, ended up chasing and capturing the six jail breakers. To honor their fallen sheriff, the people of Umatilla County had the larger-than-life statue created to sit in a small park with reflecting pools next to the highway for all to see. Sharon, my off-and-on girlfriend, was the great granddaughter of Til Taylor. There I was dating the great granddaughter of a legend and folk icon.

Following graduation at Powder Valley High I went to Weston to work in pea harvest. I worked on the bug crew, which I had done for several summers, until I was eighteen when I started working in the cannery. I was at work early and had lots of free time in the afternoon. That meant I had considerable time to spend with Sharon. She and I were having a great summer. She was now the really 'on' girlfriend and I noticed that many of my late-night dancing with April was slipping away. Sharon was real. We had seen movies in

Pendleton and Walla Walla that included: *Bridge on the River Kwai*, *Gunfight at O.K. Corral*, *Jailhouse Rock*, and the scandalous *Peyton Place*. At the drive-in in Milton-Freewater, we had seen the great movies like *Rodan* and *Love Me Tender*, the Elvis Presley classic. We had a great time at the Little Richard concert and dance. All in all, it had been a good early summer, but pea harvest was coming to an end and I would have to return to North Powder to find work. Sharon and I discussed how we were going to keep this summer going.

Sharon's grandfather and his son, Til Taylor II, had large dry-land wheat farms in the town of Athena, five miles away. Sharon knew wheat harvest would soon begin and help with harvest might be needed. She called her uncle who said he was looking for a truck driver. Sharon and I went out to his place and after a brief discussion I was offered the job. I would start in just a few days and would be staying in the 'old house,' a large two-story wooden farm house that had seen better days and was used as a bunkhouse. The migrant cat-skinner and I would sleep there. All meals would be at the main house. Sounded good, so Sharon and I were pleased. We would have more time together. Little did we know!

At the time, I did not realize I was taking part in the agricultural revolution. The ranch house I was staying in was the house of a less successful, smaller farmer and the land had been purchased and consolidated by Til. Til would eventually own a few smaller farms as he consolidated his holdings into a larger operation. The migrant cat-skinner's days were numbered. Larger and larger self-propelled combines were developed, all operated by one person in the cab. The use of a caterpillar tractor was popular and the need of a cat-skinner was drawing to a close.

Neither Sharon nor I realized or thought through the exact situation of this job. Wheat harvest took place seven days a week and did not leave any time for us to be together. Combining did not have an extremely early start as all dampness had to be gone from the grain heads before starting but there was still a great deal to do before then. First was breakfast; a big breakfast with lots of eggs, bacon, potatoes, toast, and pancakes. In the morning I had to take care of the truck and help with servicing the combine, which included cleaning the air filter, checking the oil and tires, greasing all drive-line zerks, and checking the exhaust system on the truck. During harvest time the exhaust pipes were removed and a straight exhaust, with no mufflers, went straight up beside the driver's door. This was to remove heat from the engine area as fire was a huge concern in the day of high stubble. It was very loud! On the combine, I had to check all belts and do more greasing.

The harvest day ran as late as possible for the harvest crew to still get to dinner. The harvest crew meant Til Taylor running the combine; a migrant cat skinner, who came every year, pulled the combine with a cat, and I drove truck. That meant I had to take the last load to the grain elevator with just enough time to get washed up at the 'wash house,' a separate small building that had a sink and a toilet and where I kept a clean shirt for dinner. That shirt stayed there through all of harvest and was just reused. The hours sure did not include much time with Sharon. Til and his wife were sympathetic as Sharon was his favorite niece, but little could get in the way of harvest.

Sharon's grandfather had a television at his house and every Friday night, the only exception from the harvest routine, was for the harvest crew and the extended family to meet, discuss how harvest was going, have dinner, and watch *The Gillette Cavalcade of Sports*. In 1957, that meant boxing: Championship boxing from Madison Square Garden. The voice of Jimmie Powers was always on the microphone. The theme music, "Look Sharp/Be Sharp" was played before and after each round advertising Gillette razors and blades, bringing us all to attention. Rooting for the aging Archie Moore or Émile Griffith or some other favorite boxer was part of the fun. Sharon made it over but with dinner, boxing, and family around, little time and privacy was left for Sharon and me. Shortly after dinner we returned to the barn to get an early start on the next day. Wheat harvest ended in mid-August so I was back looking for work.

I was now old enough to work in the cannery. No more peas were coming in, but large boxes of frozen peas needed to be packaged into the small retail boxes. I would empty a large box of peas, frozen into a block, onto grates over bins where they were packaged or could be mixed with other vegetables. Late in the first week, while I was pounding on a block of peas, the watch band on my new graduation Bulova watch broke. I watched as it fell down into the grinder. I yelled to stop the machine, but it was too late. My beautiful watch that was going to help me get to class on time had been ground into shreds of metal and put into the little boxes of peas. The cannery threw away lots of peas that day and I had the honor of calling home and explaining how I had destroyed the watch and ruined many boxes of peas. I wasn't charged for the peas but I knew how the folks had scrimped and saved to purchase this special watch for me. That call was not an easy one to make but it had to wait until Sunday evening when rates were lower.

Completing pea harvest, then wheat harvest, and some days at the cannery, summer rapidly came to an end. I had enough to pay for my first year of college. It had been a good summer in all respects, but Sharon and I had a problem. We did not want this romance to be just a summer romance. We did not want to break up! I was heading for Oregon State College and she was heading to a college in Washington. We had a weekend to make what we considered a very serious decision. Would one of us change schools, would we try to keep it together for later, or would we make a clean break? We both had hopes and aspirations that would be complicated by a serious relationship. Saturday night found a hillside to park and talk and talk and talk some more. I should have written the song, "Breaking Up Is Hard to Do." In 1962 Neil Sedaka wrote it; he must have heard of our pain. Sharon and I became, "Our Road Not Taken." For quite some time I danced with Sharon as the music played, "I'll See You in My Dreams."

About the Author

AFTER GRADUATING from Powder Valley High School, North Powder, Oregon, in 1957, I went on to college and graduated from Eastern Oregon College in 1961. I was a social studies teacher for 37 years at various grade levels, then retired and moved to Central Oregon to live the good life of golf and travel and seeing grandkids. Realizing my golf game was not getting any better by playing more, I decided to challenge my brain to help keep it young. Doing something different, I tried piano but found I had stone fingers.

I kept telling my wife I had dreams of stories I should write. Sometimes the story/dream lasted two weeks and sometimes longer. I had the complete outline of the story, but never did a thing about it until I saw an item in our church bulletin about writing your own story. This was being sponsored by Hospice for those who needed to get their story recorded. I thought, why not try it? They let me in the class even though I had not lost someone or was about to kick the bucket. That group became a writing group. I soon found another group that met in a book store every other week. I needed to have something fresh to read aloud to the group each week. I started writing what I knew best, the stories of my youth. Both writing groups looked forward to my stories and began encouraging me to put them together in a book. I found that my fingers still remembered the lessons learned in typing class. It became an enjoyable task. I looked forward to remembering and rehashing my stories and then one story would remind me of another story. They seemed to take on a life of their own.

Thinking through my stories I soon realized that over half of the participants were deceased and if anyone was going to get some of these stories from a different time, I had better get busy. The stories of events are all true, although sometimes I am not so sure who participated in the story. If you are one of my classmates who was there but I did not have you taking part, I apologize or if you were not there and I included you in the story, you should have been there.

I am never sure if some of the stories when I was five or six were as I remembered them or if they were talked about so often that they became part of the memory. Kind of a grey area, but they all are part of my memory. Yearbooks became an often-used source of information for the time frame of some of the stories. Five of us spent time in Enterprise trying to find dates and found very little. We heard, "We know it happened but not sure when." This is especially true of the Globetrotters story. I contacted most of my Powder Valley classmates but only got one or two responses; maybe they want the stories buried and forgotten. The town of Arlington was moved and old Arlington would be covered by the rising waters of the Umatilla Reservoir behind the new John Day Dam. For many, it was talking about two different places. I wanted the old Arlington while they knew the new Arlington.

50886987R00111

Made in the USA
Columbia, SC
14 February 2019